TIME LIFE BOOKS ®

THE ART OF SEWING
THE OLD WEST
THE EMERGENCE OF MAN
THE AMERICAN WILDERNESS
THE TIME-LIFE ENCYCLOPEDIA OF GARDENING
LIFE LIBRARY OF PHOTOGRAPHY
THIS FABULOUS CENTURY
FOODS OF THE WORLD
TIME-LIFE LIBRARY OF AMERICA
TIME-LIFE LIBRARY OF ART
GREAT AGES OF MAN
LIFE SCIENCE LIBRARY
THE LIFE HISTORY OF THE UNITED STATES
TIME READING PROGRAM
LIFE NATURE LIBRARY
LIFE WORLD LIBRARY
FAMILY LIBARY:
THE TIME-LIFE BOOK OF THE FAMILY CAR
THE TIME-LIFE FAMILY LEGAL GUIDE
THE TIME-LIFE BOOK OF FAMILY FINANCE

VANISHING SPECIES

BY THE EDITORS OF TIME-LIFE BOOKS

With an Introductory Essay by Romain Gary

TIME-LIFE BOOKS, NEW YORK

VANISHING SPECIES

Editor: Kathleen Brandes
Picture Editor: Patricia Hunt
Designers: Charles Mikolaycak, John Martinez
Staff Writer: Simone D. Gossner
Researchers: Shirley Miller, Yvonne C. Wong,
Editha L. Yango
Design Assistant: Vincent Lewis

EDITORIAL PRODUCTION
Production Editor: Douglas B. Graham
Assistant: Gennaro C. Esposito
Quality Director: Robert L. Young
Assistant: James J. Cox
Copy Staff: Rosalind Stubenberg (chief),
Reese Hassig, Florence Keith
Picture Department: Dolores A. Littles,
Jessy Faubert

Portions of this book were written by Sarah Brash. Valuable assistance in preparing the book was provided by the following individuals and departments of Time Inc.: Editorial Production, Norman Airey, Nicholas Costino Jr.; Library, Benjamin Lightman; Picture Collection, Doris O'Neil; Photographic Laboratory, George Karas; TIME-LIFE News Service, Murray J. Gart; Correspondents Maria Vincenza Aloisi and Josephine du Brusle (Paris), Margot Hapgood and Gail Ridgwell (London), Bernard Diederich (Mexico City), John Dunn (Melbourne), Elaine Handler and Rudolph Rauch (Rio de Janeiro), Peter Hawthorne (Johannesburg), Mary Johnson (Stockholm), Elisabeth Kraemer (Bonn), Robert Kroon (Geneva), Judy Leggatt (Sydney) and James Shepherd (New Delhi).

CONTENTS

PREFACE

Assembling a book on vanishing wildlife, a world of fascinating creatures perhaps doomed to disappear, can be a dispiriting task. But we approached the project with the hope that it would provoke serious concern and stimulate positive conservation activity. Within the finite limitations of this book, we have gathered a large, representative sampling of the world's rare and endangered animals. The fact that these pages cannot encompass all of the more than 1,000 creatures currently in jeopardy indicates the extent of the tragedy.

The photographs have been selected from all of the earth's zoogeographic regions. The familiar animals are here: the humpback whale, the American alligator, the southern bald eagle. So are some unfamiliar and less publicized ones: the Pine Barrens tree frog, the pygmy hippopotamus, the monkey-eating eagle.

An international list of rare and endangered mammals, amphibians, reptiles and birds —arranged as scientists classify them—appears in the Appendix, which begins on page 248. Our principal sources for this information were the International Union for Conservation of Nature and Natural Resources, the United States Department of the Interior and the 1973 Convention on International Trade in Endangered Species of Wild Fauna and Flora.

However, even a list so carefully compiled cannot be considered exhaustive; there undoubtedly are many threatened and endangered species that do not yet appear on official lists. In fact the assumption is sound that there are creatures yet undiscovered that will disappear before scientists can find and classify them.

The essay that follows introduces the plight of these vanishing animals. It was written by Romain Gary, the eminent author whose intense interest in the relationship of man and nature has been expressed often, most notably in his *The Roots of Heaven*.

—THE EDITORS

INTRODUCTION: How many warnings do we need, how much beauty gone?

There is nothing in nature to prove that it cares more for our human species than for daffodils. We may one day vanish as quickly and as radically as thousands of other breeds before us. But whatever we have in common with other living things, there is one characteristic that is our exclusive genius: we are the only species in nature working toward its own destruction.

Those who endeavor to change our ways, laboring to save this planet and its human and animal inhabitants, often pin their hopes for constructive action on our self-interest and our capacity for listening to the voice of reason. Their argument runs true: whatever man is doing against wildlife and its chances of survival, he does against himself and his own future. Nonetheless, when the case for preservation is put forward in terms of man and man alone, I find the approach a bit saddening; in my opinion, conservationists overestimate mankind's capacity for rational behavior. I see more hope for threatened species—and indeed for ourselves—in the irrational relationships between a man and his dog, an old lady and her cat, a child and his pet snake or canary. After all, nature is not something that can be separated from emotions. To save the big cats of Africa, the giant snakes, the giant panda, the kangaroo will take something more than a rational appreciation of the fact that two and two make four.

However, one of the difficulties we have when dealing with wildlife and the environment is to establish exactly where reason ends. Farming, for instance, seems a perfectly sensible endeavor, and yet it is fraught with irresponsibility. Australia, a very young and still underpopulated country, holds the most pitiful record for land, flora and fauna devastation; within three generations, nature's work of thousands of years has been annihilated by huge herds of livestock. In many places the land is unrecognizable. In Africa, large herds of cattle have inflicted wounds that can be seen easily from aircraft. Scars of bareness stretch hundreds of miles; whole regions have become deserts simply because of grazing and hoofing—that is, the stomping-out of young plants by cattle. In East Africa, the wild-animal population has dropped by 75 per cent just during our lifetime, and the area that has been capable of supporting immense wild herds for millennia has been reduced by half.

Yet the simple act of farming, and indeed many other manifestations of so-called civilization, are not inherently bad. The difficulty is knowing where to stop—and, sometimes, how best to begin. Brazil has decided to open the fabulous riches of the Amazon basin to development and industrialization. Its resources of energy and of mineral and economic wealth are enormous. The majority of Brazil's population is poor and the project will help the country become both prosperous and powerful. But the dense rain forests of the Amazon basin are the greatest reservoir of the earth's supply of life-sustaining oxygen and they provide shelter for hundreds of species of wildlife. Exploitation is therefore likely to cause far-reaching and irreparable damage.

Yet the work is well underway. And whenever this issue is raised in the world's press, Brazil's ambassadors angrily stress their country's right to self-development and often accuse those who issue the warning of trying to prevent Brazil from becoming a major power. They also point out, quite legitimately, that this thoughtfulness in matters of conflict between progress and ecology should begin at home, and that the large Western nations, so helpful with warnings and advice, are themselves the worst offenders. And so the Amazon basin will be opened to "civilization." There will be one more industrial giant in the world and the ecological consequences may then no longer necessitate theoretical studies but post-mortems.

The rationale of self-preservation *is* overwhelming and the weight of scientific evidence universally acknowledged. Our fate *is* linked to the survival of the Amazonian rain forests, the plankton in the seas, the fish in our lakes and rivers, and, by extension, the jaguar, the wolf, the grizzly bear and the bald eagle. You may not feel personally disturbed by the knowledge that more than 200 species of mammals, birds and reptiles have become extinct within the last three or four centuries, mostly through our fault, nor by the realization that hundreds of others—the gorilla, the orang-utan, the giant tortoise, the whooping crane, the big cats, the whales — will soon be found only in fairy tales unless there is something I permit myself to call a change of heart. But is it really necessary to keep on saying that no man is an island? How many warnings do we need? How many proofs and statistics, how many deaths, how much beauty gone, how many "last specimens" in those sad zoos?

Nevertheless, at the risk of passing for an idealist, I refuse to believe that the indispensable support for wildlife conservation can come only as an answer to the rationale of self-preservation. Something else is needed here, something different from hard reason. Whatever name we may give it —generosity, sense of wonder, sympathy, craving for lost innocence—it has a great deal more to do with feelings and emotions than with the dialectics of our own survival.

The problem of our vanishing species is not merely a matter of prudent husbandry of our resources. It is also a matter of loving children, nursery rhymes, toys, games, laughter and of what used to be meant by virility before this notion sank into the neurotic sexology of machismo: a need to help, to defend and to protect. Machismo is always out there with a gun—kill-

Thylacine (Tasmania)
A carnivorous marsupial, the thylacine has not been sighted since 1966 and may already be extinct. Because of its general appearance, the thylacine has been called a tiger, a wolf and a hyena, but it is unrelated to any of them.

ing for pleasure, trophy or belief. Robert Kennedy told me at Malibu, a few days before he was killed, that the saddest heritage left by Ernest Hemingway, whom he greatly admired as a writer, was the masculine mystique of the gun. It may be that my emotionalism is bad for literature; we are not dealing here with literature, however, but with the nature of our guts and with whatever is supposed to make them human.

In the Bolivian Andes I have seen a starving peasant share with his dog some food I gave him and then pick up the huge, skeletal animal and carry him up the mountain on his back. There was no rationalism there, and whatever there was goes by the name of "human." Animals thought of as something more than meat and skin are a cultural concept, as is all beauty, and such a concept cannot be dissociated from feelings. For too long, feelings have been dismissed as sentimentalism, while materialism has been exalted to the point that the world has witnessed holocaust after holocaust. Let's try sentiments and emotions for a change.

Despite all the present scars and misdeeds, the rape of the earth will not show its full, awesome consequences for perhaps two or three more generations. We could therefore go on ransacking and vandalizing our habitat without direct danger to ourselves in our lifetime—though the wild animals would surely continue to dwindle and die. What is at stake here is not what will happen to us but what will happen *after us*. And we need genuine emotion to identify with our species as a whole and with its future.

The greatest threat to both animal and human life is ignorance. Like the Australian farmer or the Brazilian developer, we are often blind to what may be happening on our own doorsteps. Last year, in the fishing village in Mallorca where I live, the catch was far below that of previous years. The head of the fishermen's association told me, "There are fewer fish this year. They don't come this way because of underwater spearfishing." He had told me the same nonsense the year before. The fact is that the fish do not come *this* way or any *other* way; the fish of the Mediterranean are on their way to extinction. The pollution of this ancient sea can be compared in its horror only to the medieval plague. The Mediterranean is becoming an oily, stinking, plastic, turgid mess: the cradle of our civilization is paying the price of our disregard for our own heritage.

The introduction of foreign species without proper study or competent advice offers an example of the terrible damage ignorance can cause. More than a hundred years ago, in 1859, the European wild rabbit was introduced into Australia by an Englishman seeking the comfort of familiar animals. *Three years later* this remarkably enterprising and prolific creature was measured as the greatest disaster ever to hit the huge country. It laid the land bare, upsetting the ecological balance. When a thoughtfully chosen disease, myxomatosis, was deliberately introduced to fight the little devils, a huge part of the rabbit population died as a result. But a few years later the rabbit was back at it again, growing in numbers, in strength and in immunity to the disease.

In the face of these—and other—blunders, let us not fall into the old trap of believing that ignorance is prevalent only among so-called savages. Savagery can take very exquisite forms. Not until 1972 did the International Fur Trade Federation even agree to a request from the World Wildlife Fund for a moratorium on trade in leopards' and cheetahs' skins. Just two decades ago, the number of vicuñas in the Andes was estimated at more than a million. The latest survey shows that perhaps 15,000 survive in remote parts of Argentina, Bolivia, Chile and Peru—inaccessible to vicuña-coat lovers.

And do I need to remind the reader of the slaughter for skins of the baby seals in Norway? It took generations before this particular bit of information reached the outside world. The outcry was tremendous, but the heartbreaking pictures keep coming out, year after year. It is quite obvious, of course, that what is being murdered is as much Man—yes, with a capital M—as seal. If we have to fall back for the billionth time upon notions of self-respect and dignity when dealing with even such a humanitarian nation as Norway, then the illiterate African hunter who depletes game through ignorance may turn out to be less threatening to our future.

We kill chickens, of course, and lambs and rabbits, so why not seals or deer or rhinos—or vicuñas? Friends, I have no answer to that, and therefore, as far as hard reason is concerned, killer takes all. The heart either speaks or it does not. The reason why has about as much to do with rationality as has beauty. If the relationship between our species and the rest of the earth's inhabitants is to be reduced to the necessities of our own survival, then we are not talking about the same man. It is absurd to cram our museums with art and to spend billions for beauty and then to let beauty be destroyed wantonly in all its living splendor. I may be mistaken, but it's too late in life for me to change my beliefs: I am convinced that we do not have to feel personally threatened by an ecological disaster to feel troubled by the news that there are no more than a hundred swamp deer left in central India. I do not even believe that we need to know exactly what the swamp deer looks like, or even how beautiful it is. I have heard Polish boys in Warsaw discuss the woeful tale of the American bison as if it weighed heavily on their non-American consciences.

I don't know if you are interested in the Ethiopian wild ass, but I am;

Jamaican Iguana
No Jamaican iguanas have been seen alive by scientists since the 1940s. After mongooses were brought into the area in the 19th Century to destroy rats and snakes, the iguana population rapidly declined. Inoffensive though they are, these ground dwellers were also killed by fearful residents.

maybe because I met one 30 years ago in Somaliland and it looked at me in a certain way that I have never forgotten. It had been badly hurt by a truck and was dying. There are only 3,000 left now. The World Wildlife Fund reports that one menace to wild asses is the tourists' practice of chasing them around to take pictures, and the animals die of exhaustion. Make your own distinction between the wild asses and the other ones.

The passionate preoccupation with species other than our own is a recent development, and this is not due to ecological awareness alone. It stems partly from disillusionment—with civilization and with ourselves—particularly among the young people. I am optimistically staking my chips on youth—that turbulent reservoir of life—and its capacity for indignation. It is indignation that makes the strength of political issues.

Our agonizing reappraisal comes at just about the right time; it is not yet too late, for either man or beast, even though one of the most amazing aspects of our "bite" on nature is the frightening speed at which the work of evolution is undone. It took life more than 100 million years to come up with the giant sea turtle, the whale and the monk seal, but it took us only three generations to reach a point where their total disappearance looks almost inevitable. This process of eradication occurs at all levels of living organisms, from the largest to the microscopic forms. Bacteria break down sewage, but the effect of chemical pollution makes their sanitary work impossible through a decline of oxygen in the water—as is already happening in the Mediterranean and elsewhere. Sooner or later, pathogenic bacteria spread disease to man and animal alike.

This aggression goes on constantly, second by second, from the top of the tree of life to its roots. There is no such thing as separate species, ecologically speaking: all breeds are interrelated—plant and animal—and all bear the consequences. And that is why the sea, that original breeder of us all, is high on the priority list of conservation.

Today nothing is further from the truth than the poet's "and the mighty ocean washes everything away." Our seas are contaminated to such an extent that Jacques Cousteau, the famous underwater explorer, warns that if we do not mend our ways, the seas will die. The fish catch of our seas and oceans drops every year, and Thor Heyerdahl, crossing the Atlantic on *Ra II*, his papyrus boat, found that the ocean was polluted hundreds and thousands of miles from the nearest land or sea routes. Sooner or later, every chemical poison finds its way into the water—and kills. It kills microorganisms—the sea's living tissue, its blood, cells, oxygen. There have been reports in the press giving the oceans 30 to 40 years to live. Although such estimates are probably exaggerated, the murderous process goes on.

There are comforting signs of awakening, however. The residents of coastal areas react angrily to the sight of beaches covered mile after mile with plastic bottles, dead fish and birds, all caught in the black glue of oil. In March of 1973, the "red mud" pollution, caused by chemicals from the Montecatini Edison plant on the western coast of Italy, became a political issue in Corsica. The French government woke up and complained to the Italian government, which promised action. I am not inciting anyone to riot, but there is no harm in twisting officialdom's ear when it plays deaf.

So, we have brutally interfered with nature through pollution, deforestation and in many other ways. How often have I heard the expression, usually uttered with a knowing smile, that "nature knows how to take care of itself"? It does indeed and it may straighten things out, but it may well achieve a new equilibrium only at the expense of the earth's most famous inhabitant and most dangerous predator.

The turning point in the worldwide concern with conservation was the publication in 1962 of Rachel Carson's deeply moving *Silent Spring*. The quality of writing and of feeling was as effective as the amount of scientific evidence put forward on page after page. The book provoked precisely the kind of popular response that occasionally prompts even governments into action. This reaction confirmed again how deeply nature and culture are interwoven in matters of conservation—and also the tragic scope of the problem, since so much of the world's population is beyond the reach of the printed word.

Silent Spring started a landslide of books on the subject and was largely instrumental in bringing forth the first decisive, long-overdue legislation and action in the field of pesticides. The director of the New York Zoological Society, William G. Conway, has described succinctly the infamous process that takes place when pesticides are used indiscriminately: "Pesticides applied to control insects on crops eventually wash into watercourses and the sea, where they are ingested by microorganisms which are themselves eaten by fish and other animals. These latter are, in turn, eaten by the birds. At each step in this food chain, the pesticide is further concentrated. One result of such concentrations is that affected birds produce eggs with shells so deficient in calcium that they are crushed in incubation. Because of this process, brown pelicans, cormorants, peregrines, bald eagles and many other birds of prey are already extinct in various localities."

Pesticide pollution has even reached Antarctica and the Arctic; the penguin and the polar bear already have been affected. Each year new names are added to the writing on the wall, with the interesting exception of rats and termites. Which of these two species is going to inherit the earth is any-body's guess. They may even be intelligent enough to reach a certain balance and agree to share it.

The fight to save our threatened wildlife cannot be won by a professional elite alone; conservationists, zoologists, ecologists and game wardens can accomplish very little without governmental and popular support. And some of the choices facing governments are awesome. As we have seen, in large areas of the earth farming has become the enemy of the soil. And yet, how can one convince the populations of countries that are in the process of development to put an end to intensive farming when all their toil and sweat keeps them barely ahead of starvation? Most of the fresh meat consumed in Ghana and in Zaïre (formerly known as the Congo) comes from game. This practice gives wildlife in these regions, and its edible species, a very limited future. Yet who can argue with the human body's craving for protein?

In mid-1973 millions faced starvation as the result of drought in Africa. But drought itself is only partly to blame, for it hit a continent already made barren in many areas by deforestation. A plan to introduce cattle breeding in West and Central Africa only led to the widespread destruction of hoofed mammals in the region. Cattle are highly susceptible to nagana, the animal form of sleeping sickness, but wild hoofed mammals are immune to the disease. The latter, however, carry the disease and host the blood-sucking tsetse flies that transmit nagana to livestock. In an effort to eradicate nagana and its carriers, and to make room for the domestic herds, there was wholesale slaughter of water buffalo, antelope and other large mammals. But the tsetse fly prevailed and the farmers' herds that were vulnerable to nagana perished. The attempt at cattle raising ended in disaster. This is but one example of mismanagement, misbehavior and ignorance committed by rational human beings.

Nonetheless, many things can still be re-established and saved—and indeed a lot is being accomplished. We must remember that only 15 to 20 years ago, the word ecology was completely unknown to the general public. Ten years ago I tried it out at a chic dinner party in Paris; among some 20 people present, only three were able to tell me its meaning. Now it pops up everywhere. The World Wildlife Fund, certainly one of the more active groups in the field, came into existence only in 1961. The International Union for Conservation of Nature and Natural Resources (IUCN), which periodically publishes an annotated list of the word's rare and endangered species (Appendix, page 248), came into existence in 1948. The first important international conservation organization, the International Council for Bird Preservation, goes back to the 1920s. The first major, widely publicized speeches on the matter by heads of state are very recent.

Considering how new our awareness is, its spread throughout all the nations of the world is more than encouraging. Most African states became independent less than 20 years ago, yet their governments are already deeply preoccupied with the problem and have taken action. In Kenya and Tanzania exemplary efforts are being made by conservationists, and the game reserves and natural parks there are both sanctuaries for wildlife and laboratories where ecological balance is studied. The whole, vast Serengeti National Park in Tanzania is an open-air university for the study of nature. And, among all the beautiful sights there, to me the most beautiful of all was a bus full of students with this inscription on its side: "Wildlife Education." Long live Tanzania!

New national parks and game reserves are, therefore, essential. Establishing them is our most urgent task right now, if only because without them there will be no vanishing species to save. Many steps have already been taken, and the dedication and good will shown by both private organizations and government officials are encouraging and sometimes admirable. Thanks primarily to a British group, the Wildfowl Trust, the population of the nene, or Hawaiian goose, Hawaii's state bird, has increased from a few specimens in 1949 to a current total of more than 1,000. There is even hope for the Arabian oryx, hunted for centuries on the Arabian Peninsula as a virility trophy and declared extinct in the wild only 10 years ago. It has now been revived in the confines of the Phoenix Zoo in Arizona and the San Diego Wild Animal Park in California. As soon as larger numbers are available, these antelope will be returned to their native habitat, where hopefully they will continue to increase—if a moratorium is declared on virility, that is.

In the U.S.S.R. the saïga antelope no longer is endangered and actually is prospering. There is even hope for kangaroos: the Australian government has been persuaded to ban all exports of kangaroo meat and hides. In 1973 the U.S. government sponsored a successful international effort to limit trade in more than 375 endangered species. It may not be too late for the California condor, though this magnificent bird, of which there were 60 in 1947, has now been reduced to a population of about 50. But I doubt that there is still hope for the green turtle or the Caribbean monk seal.

"Only about a quarter of the species of birds and mammals that have become extinct since 1600 may have died out naturally," wrote James Fisher in *Wildlife in Danger.* "Humans, directly or indirectly, may be responsible for the extermination of the rest." For this reason, the present promising

Ivory-billed Woodpecker (U.S.)
The tinny call of this 20-inch woodpecker may never be sounded again. Heavy logging in swampy areas deprived it of the wood-boring insects on which it fed and sent its population into a seemingly irreversible decline.

trend toward establishing new sanctuaries for individual species represents no more than emergency measures—giving them, and us, a breathing spell. But we must use the time intelligently.

Wilderness and wildlife depend for their continued existence on the direction of mankind's cultural development. Or, to put it another way, the quality of life—which involves the earth and every life form, the whole of the biosphere—depends on both the quality and the quantity of man.

The present population explosion is in the process of becoming a natural cataclysm and its first consequences are already apparent everywhere. Even considering only our most elementary physiological needs, the possibility of feeding the earth's population declines with the constant swelling of the demographic flood, and the very progress we are achieving in developing new sources of food and energy plays havoc with nature—air, water, soil—thus accelerating the process of depletion. This vicious circle has been formulated perfectly by my friend Georges Hansen: "The longer and better mankind lives, the worse off it will be."

Our genetic creativity is running so much out of control that our social creativity falls further and further behind it. In India alone, the industrial expansion and economic development are overtaken year after year by new increases in population. The soil and the ocean have become impoverished by the very struggle to create new resources. It is absurd to think that a limited habitat can accommodate an unlimited number of inhabitants. When the pressure on the habitat grows too great, millions of essential links between us and nature are broken in such a way that the umbilical cord on which we depend for breathing and existing is endangered. Culture is the key to survival, both for man and for the whole tree of life, which knows no privileged species. Mother Nature has no mama's darlings.

The confusions of this age, the social and moral disarray, the challenges —particularly to the young people of the world—to what once were secure traditional values have contributed, perhaps more than anything else, to this new awakening of our interest in the tree of life and all its ramifications. There is a certainty, a solid, unshakable truth to which we can cling that cannot betray us. It also offers a rare possibility for unanimous agreement in this time of bitter and bloody ideological strife.

For those who are inclined to meditate upon the good consequences of evil, I shall point out that the atomic bomb played an important and perhaps decisive role in our present concern with the environment. The nuclear experiments and the subsequent peril of radiation to men, beasts and flora alike brought ecology to the attention of the masses. It immediately became a political issue of major proportions and it is destined to remain so, particularly since the attitude of young voters on the matter is unequivocal, unforgiving and watchful. The importance of this development cannot be overemphasized. No progressive government can afford to dismiss the voice of youth. Politics may not move mountains, but it is remarkably effective in moving politicians. This explains, no doubt, why a considerable degree of international cooperation is finally being achieved.

Still, I am confident that there is something more behind this drive for the preservation of the earth and its inhabitants than an exclusive preoccupation with a continued presence on this planet. Every book on ecology reminds us that when the balance of nature is threatened, it always finds a way to restore that balance, at whatever cost. If endangered by us, nature will strike back and show no more concern for Michelangelo, Shakespeare or Mozart than for daffodils. We are dealing here with an overwhelming force, that of life itself, and we know next to nothing about it.

The only thing we do know is nature has no favorites among the species.

—ROMAIN GARY

1 MAMMALS

Two physical characteristics distinguish mammals from all other creatures: they are furry and the females produce milk. Hairiness, however, is a relative matter—it may mean the woolly coat of a polar bear or the few sensory bristles around the mouths of some whales. Contrary to common belief, mammals do not necessarily bear live young; the most primitive ones, like the reptiles from which all mammals evolved, lay eggs.

Early mammalian forms made their first, discreet appearance during the Age of Reptiles, about 180 million years ago. Through a gradual, but nonetheless steady process of differentiation and proliferation, mammals some 60 million years ago usurped preeminence from the reptiles and eventually inherited the earth.

Man, the dominant outcome of mammalian evolution, in some ways is the archenemy of the other milk-nourished vertebrates. Although his tendency to kill purely for the thrill of the hunt became intensified after the invention of firearms, archeological remains indicate that as early as 10,000 to 15,000 years ago he was slaughtering large mammals in quantities well beyond his needs for survival. In the New World alone such excessive killing by Stone Age hunters, probably aggravated by climatic change, led to the rapid disappearance of 31 kinds of large mammals, including mammoths, saber-toothed cats, long-horned bison, camels and a variety of huge beaver weighing 400 pounds.

The decline of mammalian species continues unabated today, and their departure could well deprive the world of an extraordinary living laboratory where we can study the labyrinthine paths of physical evolution and the development of behavior.

One seemingly obvious way to replenish this laboratory without walls is to breed endangered animals in zoos and then use the offspring to repopulate depleted colonies. For example, Przewalski's horses and white-fronted wallabies have been raised in sufficient numbers to justify returning some of these animals to the wild. Except in such rare cases, however, wild mammals seldom are able to breed in alien quarters; even the best-kept zoos must rely on captured wild specimens to restock their displays. A working alternative would require a dual approach: a coordinated international effort to establish natural preserves where species can multiply in familiar surroundings, coupled with a worldwide program of education devoted to the benefits of conservation.

There can be no improvement without the inhibition of man's instincts. If civilized man does indeed intelligently control his urges to hunt, to collect, to increase his acreage, he may yet save the earth's mammal population and thus preserve this incomparable mirror of his own past.

Pouched Mammals

Marsupials—or pouched mammals—constitute the most abundant wild fauna of Australia and its nearby islands. Their continent has been a world unto itself for 45 million years and, as a result, they have undergone a separate evolution.

They were among the first mammals to appear on earth, at a time when reptiles and dinosaurs still dominated it, and marsupials retain a unique reproductive system: the young, born immature, crawl up at once into a furry pouch on their mother's belly and attach themselves to one of her nipples until they are fully developed. In a few species, such as the rusty numbat, the female has no pouch, but an area of frizzled fur in which the baby nestles.

Throughout the rest of the world, most of the pouched mammals have been replaced by the more evolved placental mammals, which bear mature young. Meanwhile, the evolution of marsupials in Australia, though isolated, has paralleled the adaptations of wholly unrelated placental mammals elsewhere. Thus, Australia has pouched equivalents of cats, wolves, moles, squirrels, anteaters and many other species—with comparable behavior. In some instances, even the outward resemblances are strikingly similar.

This diversified fauna—there are over 150 species of marsupials in the Australian realm—managed to withstand 100 million years of evolution. It survived the arrival of the aborigines, who probably arrived from Asia some 30,000 years ago. But the settlement of Australia by Western man, less than two centuries ago, marked the beginning of a rapid decline. Seldom were more mistakes compounded in the colonization of a virgin land: imported cats and dogs preyed on native marsupials, sheep destroyed large areas of their grasslands by overgrazing, and plants of foreign origin overtook the flora on which indigenous species fed.

Alarmed by the plight thus visited on its natural heritage, Australia has banned hunting of several species and has established a number of preserves and national parks. The government also has encouraged the creation, when warranted, of breeding colonies for the more critically endangered animals.

Mountain Pygmy Possum
This little marsupial has been playing possum—literally—for some thousands of years. Until 1966 the species had been known only from fossil bones and was thought to be long extinct. But that year a live specimen was found in Australia's Victorian Alps. Since then a systematic search has uncovered many more of these rare mountain-dwelling mammals, including a colony in Kosciusko National Park, New South Wales.

Rabbit Bandicoot
Australian aborigines hunt this long-nosed little beast for food and adorn themselves with its fur. Suburbanites trap the bandicoot because it disturbs their gardens. They forget the animal rids its habitat of destructive rodents.

Hairy-nosed Wombat

A special reserve was recently established in eastern Queensland to protect 2,000 or so of these burrow-dwelling marsupials. But the area is subject to drought, and a single severe dry season could eliminate the entire population.

Quokka

Slightly smaller than a hare, the quokka (below) is a miniature wallaby. Aborigines, who supplied its name, used to spear hordes of these marsupials after flushing them from bushes in the coastal region of Western Australia.

Yellow-footed Rock Wallaby

Sure-footed rock wallabies live among rocky hills and cliffs, leaping from crag to crag with such agility that they have been called the chamois of Australia. They spend their nights in caves and, when disturbed, sound the alarm by thumping the ground like rabbits.

Eastern Native Cat

Only a wild stretch of the imagination can account for the name of this spotted marsupial, which looks more like an American opossum. Its diet includes poultry, wild birds, eggs, insects, rodents, rabbits, lizards and snakes.

White-fronted Wallaby

One of the smallest wallabies, the white-fronted, or Parma, variety stands only a foot high. It was presumed extinct from 1932 until 1966, when a small colony was discovered on the island of Kawau off the New Zealand coast. Some of its former Australian territory soon may be repopulated from specially bred stock, since it mates readily outside its natural habitat.

Rusty Numbat
The squirrel-like numbat lives almost entirely on termites, which its four-inch tongue gathers from the cracks and crevices of rotted wood. At night it beds down in a termite-hollowed trunk of a eucalyptus tree.

Brush-tailed Rat Kangaroo
This diminutive kangaroo, also called a jerboa, uses its prehensile tail for carrying bundles of nesting materials. It usually eats grasses and tubers but has acquired a special fondness for refuse. In zoos the males are so aggressive toward each other that they must be kept in separate cages.

Banded Hare Wallaby
Its ears are shorter than those of the true hare, but the hare wallaby, like its namesake, is known for its lightning speed and jumping skill. A nocturnal animal, it leads a solitary life browsing and nesting in woodland and heath.

Eastern Gray Kangaroo
Long exploited commercially, the eastern gray kangaroo was not protected until 1973, when export of its hide and meat was banned. But this mighty giant still is killed legally for both pet food and tourist souvenirs in Australia.

Insectivores and Bats

A family of insectivores, solenodons were rare even before they became endangered—so rare that they were presumed extinct at the turn of the century. Zoologists rediscovered them in 1907. Only two species of solenodons exist, and both are in jeopardy: the so-called Haitian variety (right) is now found mostly in the Dominican Republic, adjacent to Haiti on the island of Hispaniola; the Cuban species has retreated to remote areas of Oriente province and the Sierra Maestra, at the eastern tip of Cuba.

There is no available census of solenodons on either island. But they are extremely scarce, and their numbers are believed to be on the decline because individual sightings have been fewer in recent years. This steady depletion of solenodons is caused on the one hand by ever-increasing cultivation and urban sprawl, and on the other by the eagerness of foreign zoos to secure live specimens—a futile undertaking because few survive either the trip or captivity. Protective laws, adopted in the Dominican Republic in 1969, have had a limited effect so far, although the ban on export of these fragile creatures can be reinforced through intensive surveillance of harbors and airports. The future of the Cuban species appears more promising: not only are solenodons legally protected there, but part of their habitat is included in the Jaguani reserve, established in 1963 by the Cuban Academy of Sciences.

Though seemingly unrelated, bats are in fact descendants of a primitive group of insectivores, and most of their species still live on a diet of moths and other insects. Bats are found worldwide in huge numbers, and many families are thriving, but some varieties nonetheless are extremely rare or vulnerable. The threatened species are restricted to such small areas that a slight disturbance or modification of their environments could all but wipe out whole populations. In order to prevent such catastrophes, zoologists are urging intensive studies of their habitats and behavior, meanwhile stepping up an educational campaign to forestall one of the major threats to these retiring creatures: the inadvertent disturbance of hibernating bat colonies by cave explorers, local residents and tourists.

Haitian Solenodon (Hispaniola)
This rare insectivore, with a foot-long body and another foot of tail, is the size of a large rat. It is prized as a trophy by the islanders, who have contributed to the species' decline in order to display stuffed specimens on coffee tables and mantelpieces.

Indiana Bat (United States)

Although there are 500,000 of this species in the United States, 90 per cent of them hibernate in only a half-dozen caves in two states. If awakened prematurely by intruders, they die of starvation because the insects on which they subsist are still hibernating. Conservation plans for these mammals include the erection of gates at the entrances of their caves.

Spotted Bat (North America)

One of the rarest of the world's mammals, the spotted bat is best identified by its distinctive white markings and long, rabbit-like pink ears. It remains a scientific enigma, however, since its nesting sites have never been located. Only about 70 have been collected since the discovery of this species in the late 19th Century.

Apes and Monkeys

Man is the closest relative of apes and monkeys, yet it is man who has presented the greatest hazard to the primate world. Primitive peoples continue to hunt local species for food; developing societies rob primates of their habitat as land uses change; and the most advanced cultures have exploited primates by encouraging their capture and export, often under conditions that are not only inhumane but prejudicial to a species' survival. Precisely because primates are the most highly evolved of animals, tens of thousands have been used each year for biological and behavioral studies—and other tens of thousands are introduced into captivity to provide amusement in zoos, circuses and even private homes around the world. The number lost during capture and transport may well exceed by many times those that live to be traded.

The chimpanzees of Africa have been particularly popular with both behavioral and biological researchers, but too often the scientists have removed these apes from their homeland in order to study them closely. This has occurred despite the fact that British scientist Jane Goodall's pioneering observations of chimps in their natural habitat have demonstrated that far more reliable information about the behavioral traits of primates can be obtained by on-site research.

In recent years there has been some basis for optimism over the chances of primate survival. A number of countries that once were active in heavy primate trade have severely curtailed commercial trapping and export. Nevertheless, the long war in Southeast Asia devastated that region's indigenous primates. And even after the introduction of stiff conservation measures in some countries, the monkeys of Asia, Africa and South America have been reduced in numbers almost as drastically as the apes of Africa and Asia. In the rain forests along the Amazon, for example, a great many have fallen prey to poachers and smugglers, who do a brisk illegal trade with animal dealers in the U.S. As a result, about one in three species of apes and monkeys throughout the world is currently on the list of rare and endangered animals.

Mountain Gorilla (Africa)
Even though the mountain gorilla is the largest living primate, its size has not saved it from near-extinction. Meat of the gorilla is considered a delicacy by local tribesmen, who invade the rapidly dwindling havens of these primate giants on the rain-forested slopes of extinct volcanoes in Uganda, Zaïre and Rwanda. As recently as 1959, there were an estimated 5,000 to 15,000 of these massive apes; today only about 1,000 still live in the wild.

Pileated Gibbon (Southeast Asia)

The slender pileated gibbon is nature's most skilled ape aerialist; it hurls itself from tree to tree across distances as great as 40 feet. Shown here in captivity, a female of the species is far from its native habitat, where protection is limited to the narrow confines of Thailand's Khao Yai National Park.

Orangutan (Malaysia, Indonesia)

A baby orangutan swings exuberantly from a handy vine. Young and docile orangs top the list of primates subject to poaching, and capture almost always begins with the mother's murder. Singapore and Hong Kong, the usual outlets in Asia for orangutans—and other exotic animals—have finally banned the illicit commerce, so there still may be a future for Asia's largest primate.

Chimpanzee (Africa)
Chimpanzees are in such demand as performing mimics that the supply has fallen off alarmingly. In the wild, chimps can survive in areas as diverse as savanna and rain forest, but increasingly they are being forced into remote pockets where subsistence is marginal. Six African nations have now enacted laws against the capture of chimpanzees, and four other countries have set aside reserves for their protection.

Red Colobus (Zanzibar)
A flash of white mane hides the tawny fur of this monkey. Shy and delicate, it lives only in a small area of the Indian Ocean island of Zanzibar. More than a decade ago the Tanzanian government established the Jozani Forest Reserve to protect the species, but the population now may be as low as 150.

Woolly Spider Monkey (Brazil)
This rare New World monkey is one of six at the São Paulo Zoo. The species, protected only in a few Brazilian refuges, has never bred in captivity and no other zoo has been able to keep any woolly spider monkeys alive.

Golden Lion Tamarin (Brazil)
The squirrel-sized golden lion tamarin, or marmoset, is easily the world's most colorful primate, and also one of the rarest. It is succumbing quickly as its only habitat—a mere 350 square miles of rain forest—gives way to the suburban expansion of Rio de Janeiro.

White-nosed Saki (Brazil)
Holding a fist to its most distinctive feature, a white-nosed saki wears its characteristically timid expression. Potentially a victim of natural extinction, the saki has lost more territory to other Amazonian monkeys than to man.

Bald Uakari (Brazil)
This pink-faced New World monkey, also known as the white uakari, has been besieged by hungry hunters in its unprotected tropical habitat. The popularity of uakari meat is now the primary obstacle to the animal's survival.

Red Uakari (Brazil, Peru)
The red uakari is a shaggy cat-sized
monkey with a face as vivid as scarlet
paint; anger deepens the color. Like the
bald uakari, it is hunted by Amazonian
tribesmen, but the once-thriving export
operation appears to have been halted.

Lion-tailed Macaque (India)
As coffee and tea plantations gradually
have overtaken southern India's evergreen forests, the lion-tailed macaque,
or wanderoo, has failed to adjust. Its
reputation as a docile pet has also
helped drop the population below 1,000.

Douc Langur (Southeast Asia)
The slant-eyed douc langur is one of
the principal animal casualties of the
war in Indochina. Chemicals defoliated
the monkey's habitat and hungry foot
soldiers—as well as those out for target practice—have taken a tragic toll.

Lemurs

Standing on the evolutionary ladder just a rung below apes and monkeys, the lemurs of Madagascar are a colorful group of lower primates now unique to that island. They are also among the most threatened mammals in the world and may become extinct within a decade unless strict conservation measures are effected by the Malagasy government.

Although lemurs once existed in other parts of the world, they became extinct elsewhere because of the competition with more evolved mammals; only on Madagascar did they survive—mostly because the island was isolated for millions of years.

Madagascar, like the other land masses of the world, was once part of a single, huge continent named Pangaea that began to break up some 200 million years ago. Although Madagascar was one of the last areas to be separated, geological evidence indicates that it split off from Africa before ancestral forms of lemurs began to disperse there. Hence early lemurs had to cross open water, apparently on makeshift rafts, to reach Madagascar. Once there, they lived in splendid isolation and evolved along their own separate lines until historical times. The initial decline of the lemurs coincided with the first appearance of man on Madagascar about 2,000 years ago. Since then, they have been hunted for food, killed in ceremonial rites and gradually despoiled of their natural forest habitat.

Although a dozen or more lemur species have become extinct, Madagascar still harbors at least 20 of them, broadly classified into four groups: the dwarf lemurs; the cat-sized lemurs, which include the mongoose, sportive, black and red ruffed species; the monkey-like lemurs, such as avahis and sifakas; and the squirrel-like aye-ayes, which are in a category all their own because of their specialized front teeth and long, slender middle fingers.

The aye-ayes, with a wild population of less than 50—there are none in captivity outside Madagascar —are causing the greatest concern. The best hope for their survival and that of the other lemurs rests on the intense efforts of French zoologist Jean-Jacques Petter and others to establish vest-pocket preserves where they can live undisturbed.

Western Woolly Avahi
A wide-eyed threesome of avahi lemurs huddles on a tree branch. No bigger than house cats, they have woolly coats and are strictly nocturnal. They spend most of their lives aloft in the forest, but on occasion they descend to explore the ground in a brief, erect walk.

Mongoose Lemur

Smallest of the typical lemurs, the mongoose—which is unrelated to the Asian and African carnivores of the same name—lives in family groups of no more than three or four members. It is among the few lemurs that tame easily and survive well in captivity.

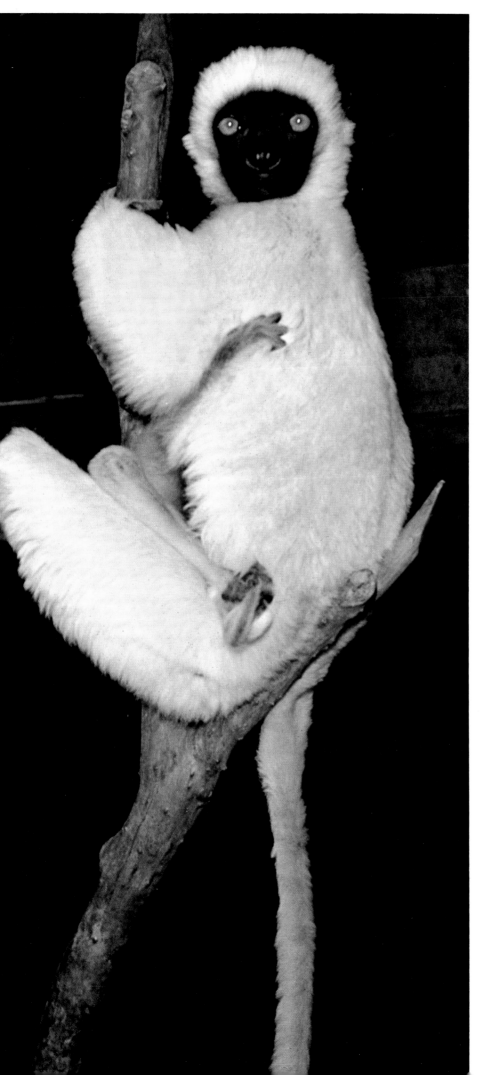

Verreaux's Sifaka
This lemur, shown with its three-month-old infant, is most active during the daytime. The name sifaka derives from the sound of the contented hiccup (see-fak) that the animal emits following a feast of leaves, bark, flowers, fruits and young plant shoots.

Black Lemur
Despite the name, only the male of the species is black; the female (above) is reddish brown. The animals, traveling in bands of 10 to 15, are most active in the morning and early evening. At night they meet in larger groups.

Nossi-bé Sportive Lemur
This saucer-eyed creature is entirely nocturnal and spends each day sleeping in a tree, curled up in a ball. Although easily captured when asleep, the species is too fragile to survive outside its natural habitat in Madagascar.

Lesser Mouse-Lemur

Shown here almost life-sized, the less-er mouse-lemur is the smallest primate still extant. Adults are only five inches long, not counting the tail, and the young measure barely an inch at birth. A typical family of four can be cradled comfortably in the palm of a hand.

Red Ruffed Lemur
This woolly creature shares with other lemurs a taste for flowers, fruit and seeds, but it is more inclined to round-the-clock activities. The deep, humid forests of Madagascar resound at almost any hour with its raucous cries.

Aye-Aye
Once a member of a large zoological family, the aye-aye of Madagascar is the most primitive of living primates and the only surviving species of its particular lemur group. It was thought to be extinct in the mid-1950s, after an absence of 24 years, but was rediscovered in 1957. Local taboos once protected this creature, but superstition has given way to civilization and little hope remains for the aye-aye's future.

Toothless Mammals

The Latin name *Edentata,* or "toothless," which has been applied by scientists to a group of New World mammals, is a curious misnomer. Among the armadillos, sloths and anteaters that constitute the group, only the anteaters have no teeth. Paradoxically, some armadillos have more—even as many as 90 —than any other mammalian species. Through an evolutionary lapse, however, their incisors and canines usually are missing, and the molars are misshapen and lack enamel.

Toothless mammals—or edentates—are the living relics of the Western Hemisphere. The southern half of the New World was in essence an island-continent for about 100 million years, and its early mammalian fauna was left to evolve separately. Edentates were among the most primitive creatures that evolved there. Later, after the Panama land bridge rose from the ocean, some edentates migrated northward to Mexico and the southern United States, where most of them became extinct.

Although they are linked by common ancestors, toothless mammals actually are a rather disparate lot. Giant anteaters have an enormous bushy tail that they can spread over themselves like a blanket; three-banded armadillos are so secure when rolled up that only jaguars and maned wolves can crack them open; and sloths are so sluggish that their average speed may not be more than 14 feet per minute, and it is usually considerably less. It has been observed that sloths even sneeze slowly.

A bear-sized sloth, now extinct, was still around when man first arrived in the Americas. Fossil findings indicate that the beast was trapped, slain and barbecued. Patagonian Indians may have domesticated it. Today these edentates are considered a poor morsel and no one is hunting them commercially. But they share the general plight of South American wildlife, as several countries—notably Brazil—cut deeply into their forests to allow for human expansion. Few of these countries show any particular concern for their natural heritage: the three-banded armadillo is one of Brazil's most endangered species, yet hunting of the animal is not prohibited by the Brazilian authorities.

Giant Anteater (Latin America)
A female anteater carrying piggyback young prowls her native savanna for ant and termite nests. This animal, which grows to more than six feet in length, uses its powerful forelimbs to rip open insect nests and its foot-long sticky tongue to lap up the bugs. Although it is severely threatened, the giant anteater is unprotected through most of its range.

Maned Sloth (Brazil)
Sloths spend most of their lives hanging upside down from tree branches, moving about with excruciating slowness. Their scruffy fur, which they never groom, harbors colonies of green algae and mothlike insects. This rare mammal has never survived longer than several months in captivity.

Three-banded Armadillo (Brazil)
There are now fewer than 100 of the rare three-banded armadillos in central and northeastern Brazil. When in danger, the animal rolls itself up into a tight ball, neatly tucking in its head and tail so that only the tough armor shows.

Rodents

Rodents live on every continent of the world, but most of their rare and endangered species—including beavers, chinchillas and porcupines—are confined to widely separated regions of the New World and of the western Pacific Ocean. Of those areas, the United States has some of the most vulnerable, little-known rodent groups.

One of those in greatest peril is the harvest mouse found only in the salt marshes rimming San Francisco Bay. This tiny creature, with its distinctive dark-brown fur, is old at the age of one year. It mates twice in the course of that year, the males courting with thin, high-pitched calls. Salt-marsh harvest mice live an isolated life, far from human habitation, and build small masterpieces of spherical nests made of grasses. Though not hunted or destroyed as pests, they gradually are losing their home grounds through land fills and the diking of salt marshes—a procedure that prevents them from returning to the safety of dry terrain at high tide.

Utah prairie dogs—actually a species of ground squirrel—have always lived in that state's high plateau country in burrows that cover many acres. The animals are feared locally because their fur is subject to infestation by plague-carrying fleas—a fairly common occurrence among furry wild beasts. Utah prairie dogs also are beset by poisoning programs motivated by their damage to crops and are now confined to 48 isolated colonies—or dog towns —whose populations total fewer than 6,000.

Texas kangaroo rats, like the true kangaroos, have powerfully developed hind legs that form a balancing tripod with their cylindrical tails, allowing them to progress in bounding leaps. They burrow extensively in the hard clay soil of low mesquite brushland, stashing away winter stores of seeds and grain. Because of their restricted choice of habitat, they currently are vulnerable to the clearing of mesquite from rangelands.

In a last-minute attempt to save all three breeds from complete extinction, U.S. conservationists are recommending that small preserves be set aside within their former range, thus ensuring the survival of these small mammals.

Salt-Marsh Harvest Mouse (California)
This dainty three-inch creature trails a three-and-one-half-inch tail. Dwelling only in salty marshlands, it is one of the few mammals able to drink salt water. But much of the water is now polluted and the bright-eyed rodent is becoming increasingly rare.

Texas Kangaroo Rat (U.S.)
A Texas-sized specimen, this rodent is as big as a house cat and far larger than any other rat within a hundred miles of its Texas and Oklahoma rangelands. It has an inch-long swatch of distinctive white fur at the end of its tail, and cheek pouches for carrying foodstuffs to its winter stock pile.

Utah Prairie Dog (U.S.)
Among the most social of animals, Utah prairie dogs live in large colonies, sheltered in vast underground galleries. If disturbed, these small white-tailed rodents have been known to abandon their subterranean homes overnight.

Small Carnivores

The sleek bodies, alert faces, pricked ears and silky coats of small carnivores usually arouse the same warmhearted popular response that domesticated cats and dogs generate in our everyday life. Nevertheless, the outlook for the future of these small wild creatures is decidedly gloomy.

The skin trade has finally been curtailed, but not without near-casualties; it is almost too late to rescue many of the small fur-bearing carnivores. The demand for their attractive pelts has always been even greater than that for skins of the larger cheetahs and leopards, because a fashionable coat requires so many more skins from, say, an ocelot or a typically small clouded leopard. In the ocelot's case, this situation is compounded by the fact that its fur comes in such a great variety of shades and markings that matching is difficult.

Regulation of the fur industry has eased one problem, but there has been no letup in the killing of small carnivores, since most of them will attack livestock when no natural prey is available and they are hungry enough. The immediate reaction of farmers and ranchers to such depredations is to gun the animals down from horses, from trucks, from airplanes. Wholesale retaliatory campaigns have already reduced such creatures as the northern kit fox, the Spanish lynx and the northern Simien fox to the status of near-extinction—fewer than 100 of each species are left. Several others are sure to be added to the critical list within a few years.

Madagascar's wildlife situation is yet another pathetic story, since animals in every category are imperiled there, primarily by a shrinking habitat. Forest-dwelling creatures like the fossa and the Malagasy civet are having more and more trouble locating the virgin forest they require for subsistence. Second-growth, or planted, forests never regain the density and variety of uncut jungle, and they are more likely to contain exotic vegetation to which the animals are unable to adapt.

To cap their difficulties, small carnivores, like so many other mammals, have disappointing records for breeding in captivity and will never be able to recoup their losses through this approach.

Ocelot (Western Hemisphere)
Ocelots are a zoological puzzle: they come in such a wide range of sizes, markings and colors that scientists debate whether they should be divided into several species. The trade in their furs has reduced their ranks, but these nocturnal animals adapt so readily to new habitats that they have a better than average chance for survival.

Spanish Lynx (Spain)
This feline once ranged through most of the Iberian Peninsula, but its attacks on domesticated stock led to its widespread persecution and wanton slaughter. The few dozens now left have been forced to retreat to protected marshlands and inaccessible mountains in the southern part of Spain.

Black-footed Cat (Southern Africa)
Smallest of the wild cats, this shy nocturnal creature is only 14 inches long—including a stubby six-inch tail. It reserves at least some friendliness for domestic cats, with which it mates, thus hybridizing the species.

Northern Kit Fox (United States)
The northern kit fox—shown here in captivity—may be extinct in the wild. It feeds mostly on insects, rabbits and small rodents, but has nevertheless been trapped, poisoned or hunted for feasting occasionally on chicken.

Fossa (Madagascar)
This oddly primitive small carnivore combines features of cats, civets and mongooses. Because it kills domesticated fowl, conservation measures include advice to Madagascar's farmers on the building of predator-proof henhouses.

Black-footed Ferret (North America)
One of the rarest mammals in North America, the black-footed ferret is wholly dependent on prairie dogs (page 70) for its survival: they are its natural prey, and their burrows are its home. The wholesale poisoning of prairie dogs has simultaneously brought the ferret to the very edge of extinction.

Malagasy Civet (Madagascar)
When fully grown, this spotted carnivore is slightly more than two feet long — tail included. It lives only near streams in the dense rain forests of its island habitat and feeds by night on small water creatures.

Otter Civet (Southeast Asia)

Although unrelated to the otter, the otter civet strongly resembles it, even to the webbing of the toes. It lives along rivers and preys on fish or thirsty birds from a submerged position with only its nostrils above water.

Clouded Leopard (Asia)

Although it has stubby legs and seldom weighs more than 50 pounds, this feline overcomes its size disadvantage by pouncing on unsuspecting animals from overhanging branches. The leopard's skin is greatly prized, but its saber-like fangs also are popular in Malaysia as ear ornaments.

Northern Simien Fox (Ethiopia)

This hapless animal has been hunted relentlessly ever since the mid-1960s because of an unsupported rumor that it was killing sheep. Ethiopia's Simien Mountains National Park, created—too late—in 1969, shelters only a remaining handful of the species.

Brown Hyena (Southern Africa)

Found today almost exclusively in national parks and game preserves, this carnivore weighs no more than 125 pounds and has long, thick fur with a handsome ruff. Its voice, far from resembling the "laugh" of larger hyenas, sounds like the hoot of an owl.

Large Carnivores

The magnificent beasts classified as large carnivores are found on every continent except Australia and Antarctica. Because of their exotic beauty, many have served over thousands of years as status symbols to the powerful and the rich.

Cheetahs were depicted on the interior walls of Egyptian tombs, Roman patricians kept them as pets, and Louis XI of France issued an edict that in his kingdom no man but himself could own a cheetah. Indian tigers, too fierce to tame, were the challenging game preferred by maharajahs and British colonials, who vied with each other in large hunting forays that yielded as many as a thousand victims to a single expedition. In recent decades the skins of leopards and other spotted cats have been prized by women who equate possession of a leopard coat to ownership of a Rolls-Royce—and are willing to pay an equivalent price.

Meanwhile, the expansion of farms and grazing land has progressively reduced the large carnivores' territories. The gradual disappearance of the carnivores' wild prey has caused them to feed on whatever livestock is at hand. The game of the rich thus became the plague of the farmers and ranchers who fought back by hunting the animals, trapping them, poisoning them. The farmers' onslaught, in combination with poaching and loss of habitat, has swept some large carnivores to the brink of extinction. Protective measures have been belated and in some cases too weak to reverse the trend: two of the "natural preserves" in India actually are little more than convenient poaching grounds.

Happily for many species, however, it is not yet too late. The panda and the maned wolf, to consider just two, remain extremely rare but their numbers seem fairly stable, at least for the moment.

In general, threatened carnivores are benefiting from a world-wide effort by conservationists to provide greater protection in the wild. Large carnivores breed poorly in captivity, and even when breeding is successful, there is little hope of reintroducing the offspring into their natural habitats. Thus, closely supervised wildlife sanctuaries offer the best prospects for survival of the dwindling species.

Florida Cougar (United States)
There are approximately 15 subspecies of the cougar, also known regionally as puma, panther or mountain lion. Of these, the Florida variety has decreased most drastically, since it has been hunted mercilessly for years. No more than 100 of them are left, and now they are found principally in Florida's Everglades National Park, where they have been fully protected since 1966.

Snow Leopard (Asia)

This medium-sized feline, gentle and friendly in captivity, is cursed with one of the most magnificent, rare and desirable of pelts. Seldom sighted, it was first photographed in the wild (left) by zoologist George B. Schaller in 1970.

Asiatic Lion (India)

The domain of the Asiatic lion was once so wide that the Bible mentions it more than 130 times. But widespread use of firearms has gradually reduced its range to the Gir Forest of western India where fewer than 200 survive.

Leopard (Africa, Asia)
These durable beasts eat anything from insects to giraffe calves and thrive anywhere from tropical forests to the cold Himalayas. Their extraordinary adaptability may well save them from the near-extinction threatened by the fur trade: since protection was provided in 1970, they have begun to increase.

Jaguar (Western Hemisphere)
The deep roar of the jaguar, largest cat of the New World, spreads terror because it attacks anything from alligators in the rivers to monkeys in the trees. It also uses its paws to scoop fish out of the water after first attracting them (according to some observations) by swishing its tail as bait.

Cheetah (Africa, Asia)
Three sleek cheetahs at an East African water hole confirm the animal's reputation as the world's most handsome cat. It is also the swiftest mammal, capable of running at 60 miles per hour in 25-foot bounds. The cheetah is now almost extinct in Asia, and its African population may be as low as 10,000—found in small pockets scattered throughout the continent.

Indian Tiger (South Asia)
The Indian tiger, once an exotic feature in romantic accounts of life in India, has declined by 90 per cent since the turn of the century. Although census-taking is difficult because the animals are nocturnal and tend to travel great distances, it is estimated that only about 2,000 remain in the wild.

Maned Wolf (South America)
An extremely shy and rather fragile denizen of marshlands and savannas, the maned wolf (shown here in captivity) has long, spindly legs that enable it to move easily through tall grasses. The species has always been rare —numbering only a few thousand—and is thus particularly vulnerable to any significant change in its environment.

Wolf (Northern Hemisphere)
Classified as a pest in most of the countries of the Northern Hemisphere where it once roamed widely, the common gray, or timber, wolf is nearly extinct except in the relatively inaccessible wilds of Canada, Alaska and the U.S.S.R. Powerful and intelligent, it exhibits social behavior that includes division of labor within the pack.

Giant Otter (Amazon Basin)
This lithe creature, gulping a fish in midstream, averages five to six feet from the tip of its nose to the end of its tail. Giant otters are believed to be monogamous and to mate for life. Curious and noisy, they are an easy target for trappers, who may get as much for an otter's pelt as they do for a jaguar's.

Red Wolf (United States)

The red wolf, despite its name, has more gray fur than red and looks remarkably like an oversized coyote. Its original range, which covered much of the southeastern United States, was gradually narrowed to the coastal marshes of Texas and Louisiana by predator-control programs in the 1930s. Today the greatest threat to the survival of the species is the fact that the few red wolves remaining breed readily with coyotes and are steadily losing out to a hybrid race.

Spectacled Bear (Andes)

Highly intelligent, this 300-pound member of the bear family is the only one native to South America, where it favors the foothill forests of the Andes, often above 10,000 feet. The spectacled-bear population has fallen to a worrisome low, but is still doing fairly well in those areas of Ecuador that have not yet been deforested.

Giant Panda (Western China)

This winsome six-foot animal makes its home in the mountainous bamboo forests of Szechwan province. The region is so remote that the giant panda has yet to be studied or even accurately counted in the wild. Although classified among the carnivores because of common ancestry, pandas live mainly on enormous amounts of bamboo. The rare creatures are protected by the Chinese government.

Aquatic Mammals

Two characteristics differentiate aquatic mammals from all other mammals: they must live in or near water and they must swim to find their food. Thus most of them share the threats of water pollution, indiscriminate hunting in international waters, human invasion of their nesting beaches and loss or destruction of their natural food supplies.

They are, nonetheless, a diverse group with unexpected and often appealing personality traits. Few sights are funnier than a sybaritic sea otter afloat on its back, carefully anchoring itself to a strand of kelp before taking a nap. The shapeless manatee, for all its homeliness, is a devoted parent; the playful humpback whale sings with such uniqueness of tone and meter that its elaborate improvisations have inspired folk singers and composers alike. On the other hand, few battles are bloodier than those fought between male elephant seals at matingtime.

Aquatic mammals have been victimized for generations by inadequate and archaic international regulations governing their capture. Where agreements have been reached among sovereign countries, the accords have not always been honored, particularly since many nations have a large economic stake in the status quo.

The whaling industry—which has come a long way since the days of Moby Dick—has developed sophisticated factory ships that take care of every phase of the hunt, from electronic detection to hauling the catch aboard to processing the last ounce of precious ambergris. One of the few hopes for the future lies with the International Whaling Commission, which promises closer surveillance of catches on the high seas, although its quota system thus far has been notably ineffective.

The outlook for most fur-bearing aquatic mammals has indeed improved in recent years. Once hunted extensively for their valuable pelts, they are now fully protected and show signs of surviving. However, one emerging problem—for once—is not man-made: the warming trend of the earth's climates over the past few decades has been gradually shrinking the Arctic icecap, thereby reducing the polar bear's domain and its hunting grounds.

Northern Elephant Seal
Two male elephant seals face off in the annual competition for the affections of chosen females. These three-ton creatures were hunted almost to extinction for their oil in the 19th Century, but the resultant scarcity caused a decline in interest. Although they are still not out of danger, the protection afforded the seals has allowed them to make a comeback in recent years.

Humpback Whale
At home in both the Atlantic and the Pacific, humpback whales commute between cool waters in the summertime and tropical areas in winter. They gambol and splash, creating huge sprays of white water, and give voice to a repertoire of eerie tunes that range from deep bass to high ultrasonic notes.

Hawaiian Monk Seal
A cowl-like fold at the back of the neck gives the monk seal its name. Although gentle and tame, it shuns humans and tends to retreat to deserted beaches. The species inhabits the chain of reefs and atolls stretching northwest of the main Hawaiian Islands.

Southern Sea Otter
Protected in California, the southern sea otter seldom strays from the kelp beds that harbor its favorite food: abalone. To get the meat, an otter will float on its back and crack open the abalone's shell by banging it against a rock balanced on its chest.

Polar Bear
These huge carnivorous mammals live on pack or drift ice where seals are found. In pursuit of their dwindling favorite prey they will swim for many miles or follow the drift of the ice around the North Pole. During the short Arctic summer, when the ice melts, they return to the land, there to subsist on berries, roots, carrion and—with luck —some Eskimo's meat cache.

Galápagos Fur Seal
Shy and retiring, Galápagos fur seals rarely stray from the sea caves and shaded ledges of the Pacific where they find shelter. They were destroyed in such numbers by 19th Century sealers that eventually it became uneconomic to hunt their greatly depleted colonies. This fortuitous circumstance has allowed them to make a gradual recovery in some Galápagos coastal areas.

North American Manatee
A close relative of Mediterranean sirenians—the mermaids of ancient lore— the manatee hardly shares the elegant, slender shape of the mythical figures; it is too bulky even to haul its own 1,000-pound heft ashore. The manatee's predilection for narrow inland waterways frequently brings it into the lethal range of motorboat propellers.

Elephants

Thousands of years ago woolly mammoths and mastodons ranged over much of the earth, including the arctic wilds of Siberia and Alaska. But elephants, their modern descendants, are adapted only to the tropics of Asia and Africa.

Africa's elephants—larger and less tractable than those in Asia—may run out of space in a few decades, as farms and villages usurp more and more·of their grazing lands.

Although elephant hunting has been banned in a few African countries, Asia's elephants are far more imperiled: in the last 400 years Ceylon elephants alone have declined 90 per cent from a total of 40,000. The threat to their survival throughout Asia was caused originally by agricultural enclaves that fragmented their forests and grasslands. Their peril was particularly intensified in Ceylon (now Sri Lanka) by the misguided belief among the island's elephant handlers that captive elephants lose their strength if allowed to mate. When the supply of domesticated elephants waned, the handlers merely took to the forests to capture more wild specimens.

Easily tamed and remarkably intelligent, Asian elephants have long been trained to perform elaborate tasks. More than 800 years ago, they hauled giant logs to clear the forest for the famous Cambodian temples at Angkor Wat, and even today the maneuverable beasts are used instead of bulldozers in otherwise impenetrable jungle areas.

The Asian elephant's life in the wild is ruled by a tightly knit matriarchal system. Youngsters stay with their mothers until they are about eight years old, and they are attended virtually around the clock during their early years. The mothers have a convenient form of day-care center. Adult elephants have such high metabolisms that they must eat almost continuously, 18 hours each day. While the herd is off foraging, the mothers take turns looking after the assembled babies.

In their endless search for food and water, the animals often stray beyond the boundaries of their reserves and easily fall prey to hunters and farmers. Thus, the most urgent need is to enlarge the existing parks by adding adjoining land.

Asian Elephant
An increasingly rare sight, a small herd of wild elephants ambles through a marshy clearing in Wilpattu National Park, Sri Lanka (formerly Ceylon). Ceylon elephants are the most seriously endangered of Asia's elephants; their range is severely limited and only three small refuges provide protection.

Odd-toed Hoofed Mammals

These ungulates belong to an assorted and widespread order of herbivores that encompasses such disparate creatures as two-ton rhinoceroses, shy tapirs, graceful zebras, wild asses and wild horses. Equipped with three toes on each of their hind hoofs, they were once abundant throughout Eurasia, Africa and South America. But modern times have brought sophisticated hunting technology, and several species are succumbing to the onslaught.

Mountain zebras, wild asses and wild horses are beautifully adapted to steppes, deserts and arid mountains. But man, who can adapt to and conquer even the most inhospitable terrain, has moved into the Asian and African homelands of these mammals, bringing along his domesticated sheep and cattle. The alien animals have driven their wild relatives from the few springs and streams, appropriated the best grazing lands and pushed the former inhabitants into even harsher environments.

In theory, the wild animals are protected by laws that prohibit hunting them. Asian wild asses and Cape mountain zebras enjoy the relative safety of preserves, but African wild asses and the remnant of Przewalski's horses in the Mongolian desert urgently need sanctuaries.

Rhinoceroses also have been hunted for centuries —often for nothing more than their horns. Pulverized rhino horn, prized as an aphrodisiac and an antitoxin in the Orient, brings poachers as much as $75 an ounce. The great Indian rhino is down to a population of about 700, existing for the most part in nine sanctuaries in India and Nepal. Africa's black rhinoceros (right) is faring only slightly better: there are several thousand left in the wild, restricted primarily to national parks in Kenya and Tanzania. If poachers and tribal herdsmen can be kept at bay, they have an even chance for survival.

The tapirs are the primitive ugly ducklings of the group. The existence of such distinctive creatures as these in regions as far apart as Latin America and Asia firmly supports the argument that the continents drifted apart millions of years ago. But as forests everywhere fall increasingly to the saws of loggers, these ancient mammals, too, will disappear.

Black Rhinoceros (Africa)
The formidable horns, armor-like hide and great bulk of the black rhino make it virtually invulnerable to would-be animal predators. But such an imposing defense proved no protection from the weapons of Europeans who considered the animal a nuisance and systematically exterminated it from the areas around their colonial settlements.

Great Indian Rhinoceros (South Asia)
Seemingly fierce but actually shy and inoffensive, a great Indian rhinoceros heads for its daily mud wallow. Such jaunts are becoming longer as farmers drain the reedy, swampy areas required by the rhino for food and cover.

Asian Tapir (Southeast Asia)
Though endangered, this nocturnal animal is not defenseless; its coloring provides camouflage in the dim jungle light. Folklore has added extra protection: tapir meat is edible, but a superstition suggests it causes leprosy.

Baird's Tapir (Latin America)
This tapir haunts dense virgin forests as far south as Ecuador. The inhospitable, rainy environment is probably responsible for the animal's survival up to now, since it has very poor sight—a defect that facilitates capture.

Asian Wild Ass (Middle East)

The wild ass, or onager, once was one of Asia's most common hoofed mammals: a Persian onager reportedly bore Christ into Jerusalem on Palm Sunday. Only about 1,000 of the Persian variety exist today, the majority of them in a game preserve in the southern U.S.S.R. The rest are in neighboring Iran, where hunters defy the law and kill the animals for their tasty meat.

African Wild Ass (Africa)

An African wild ass sprints to safety across its parched Ethiopian grazing ground. But its speed is not always adequate. Tourists in cars, hoping for a close-up photograph, frequently chase their subject, causing it to die later of exhaustion. Local Muslim tribesmen have also contributed to its decline, since the Koran prescribes ass's flesh as a cure for disease.

Przewalski's Horse (Mongolia)
Named for the 19th Century Russian explorer who first identified the species, Przewalski's horse is the only surviving unhybridized wild horse. The few animals remaining in their natural habitat live in Mongolia's desert region and neighboring uplands. Breeding in captivity has been unusually successful, but the zoo-bred offspring have not yet been returned to the wild.

Cape Mountain Zebra (South Africa)
Smaller than their more familiar cousins that live in other parts of the continent, Cape mountain zebras are about four feet tall when fully grown. Although there are only about 170 left, hunting permits still are issued to South African farmers who suspect zebras are damaging their crops.

Even-toed Hoofed Mammals

This group of ungulates, with either two or four toes on each foot, has long given man an abundance of domesticated animals—cattle, sheep, goats, camels and yaks. In addition, wild members of this order have benefited man economically, providing wool for clothing, leather for shoes and saddles, and meat for food. But in entirely too many countries and cultures, man seems intent on doing away with them, apparently not realizing that he will be the poorer.

In the wild, they are hunted indiscriminately, despite a multitude of laws. Often the hunters, though primarily interested in food, are also improvident: Saharan nomads, for instance, have been known to massacre entire herds of antelope to eat only a few. The nomads spare not even the pregnant females or calves that would supply meat for the following year. Even less explicable are the sportsmen who swell with pride when they bring down a rare specimen merely for its horns. Besides the shared danger of being hunted, these animals face the slower death that inevitably accompanies habitat destruction. As their food supply shrinks, they simply starve to death or succumb to diseases that their poorly nourished bodies cannot fight off.

These mammals also have been victims of warfare. Most recently, bombing and defoliation in Vietnam killed many wild cattle and wrecked their forest homes. During the African campaigns of World Wars I and II, antelope and wild goats were killed for fresh meat for troops.

However, man's political upheavals can sometimes provide unexpected boons for the animals. In Palestine before 1948, the Arabs and the British administrators, both avid hunters, brought much of the country's wildlife to the point of extinction. When Israel was established, some of these species began to recover, since Jews are restricted from eating the flesh of cloven-hoofed animals. In 1969 Israel created a reserve in the Negev to be a menagerie of creatures mentioned in the Old Testament. Although many of the endangered Biblical species are found today only in the Arab countries, the Israelis continue to hope that one day they will be able to complete their modern-day Noah's ark.

Dorcas Gazelle (Middle East)
The remote terrain of Israel's Negev and of northern Arabia long provided refuge for the dorcas gazelle. But these areas are now more accessible to autoborne "sportsmen," who frequently mow down the animals with powerful rifles and leave the corpses behind. One desperate Bedouin, reporting such a slaughter, said: "This was not sport. Now there are none left for me when I need one for the pot."

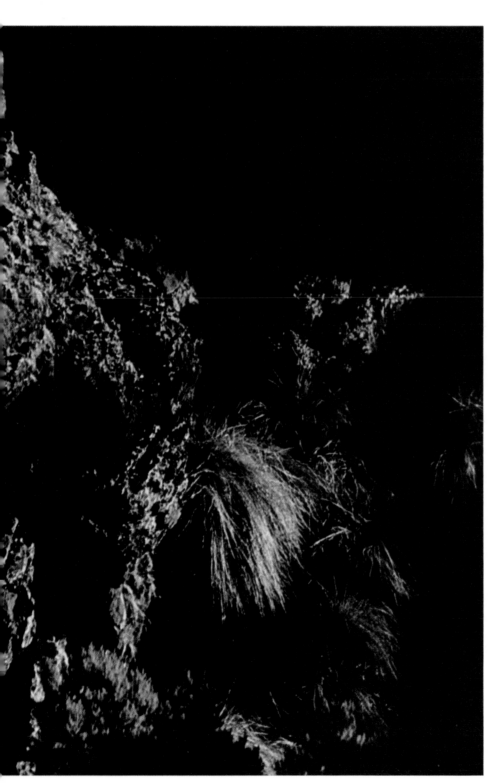

Walia Ibex (Ethiopia)
A lone walia ibex perches on a cliff hung with giant heath in the spectacularly rugged Simien Mountains. These rare wild goats range relatively undisturbed in summer in the high alpine regions; but the once richly forested lower flanks of the mountains where they winter have been largely usurped by farmers and lumbermen.

Black Lechwe (Zambia)
A black lechwe splashes through the grassy sea of the vast Bangweulu flood plain. Here the waters from 20 rivers pour into a 100-mile-wide basin to create a fertile, marshy habitat for a population of about 15,000 lechwe.

Slender-horned Gazelle (Africa)
Rolling dunes hide the hunter and muffle his steps when he stalks this desert gazelle. When he catches a fawn it cries for its mother, and he kills her as she tries to aid her young. Nowhere is the endangered animal protected.

Jentink's Duiker (West Africa)
This little forest-dwelling antelope is one of the rare specimens in captivity. It is called a duiker, or diver, because Dutch settlers in South Africa observed its relatives diving for cover at the slightest disturbance. The extreme shyness of the Jentink's duiker largely accounts for the dearth of information about its habits in the wild.

Pygmy Hippopotamus (West Africa)
A sharp-eyed hunter can travel for days in the West African jungle and see no sign of the rare pygmy hippo. The size of a large pig, this shiny-skinned mammal rests during the day and plods about at night seeking fruits and leaves. It breeds fairly well in captivity, a fact that may save it from extinction.

Swamp Deer (India, Nepal)
Easy to capture in their native grasslands and open forests, these deer have frequently fallen victim to poachers, who peddle their spiraled antlers to local boatbuilders for use as screws. Although the meat of the swamp deer, or barasingha, is tough and strongly flavored, this fact has proved no deterrent to hungry hunters.

Gaur (Asia)
The deep roar of a male gaur (far left) is even louder than the bellow of a Jersey bull. Diseases contracted from domesticated livestock have nearly exterminated these wild cattle, once common in glades and dense forests.

Bontebok (South Africa)
The bontebok (below) would have become extinct had not some 19th Century Boers given it sanctuary. About 900 of these antelope live on farms and in three reserves, a hopeful increase from the 1927 population of 121.

Bighorn Sheep (North America)
Western pioneers regarded the bighorn sheep as either a pest or a source of meat, and by 1900 a population once in the millions had been reduced to fragmented groups. Herds in the U.S. and Canada now are protected by law.

Markhor (Eurasia)
A female markhor eyes the fine, gnarled horns of a male. Because domestic goats have overrun the more accessible mountain pastures, these wild goats are desperate for food and may even climb trees to reach the leaves.

Nilgiri Tahr (India)
This mountain-dwelling goat feeds in the cool mornings and evenings; during the day it rests, while several females keep watch over the herd. Despite such vigilance, hunters have ravaged the species, and there are now only about 1,500 Nilgiri tahr.

Addax (Sahara)
The addax thrives in the bleakest parts of the Sahara, getting its water from sparse vegetation. Moving easily over the dunes on splayed hoofs, the addax is not swift enough to outrun camels bearing the hunters who have forced it toward extinction.

Mountain Gazelle (Africa, Middle East)
The embodiment of grace, the mountain gazelle moves in effortless leaps and bounds over the terrain. A great swath of country—from the Atlas Mountains on Africa's Mediterranean coast to the mountains rimming the Arabian Peninsula—once was alive with these animals. Now hunting, difficult to police in such remote areas, has reduced the gazelles to a scattered few.

Vicuña (Andes)
The silky coat of the vicuña imperils this Andean species. The Inca sheared the animals in vast seasonal roundups but they released most of them to grow more wool. Deeming it less bother to shear them dead, the Spaniards killed vicuñas by the tens of thousands. Though many countries have banned trade in vicuña wool, it still finds its way into the fashion market.

Scimitar-horned Oryx (Africa)
Overgrazing by livestock has been turning the Sahara's once-grassy fringes, home to these antelope, into true desert at the rate of about 250,000 acres a year. Unadapted to desert conditions, these elegant oryxes now must find their food closer and closer to civilized areas. Poaching goes unchecked, and only Chad has established a semidesert reserve for this species.

Wild Yak (China)
Dwindling herds of yaks have retreated to the barren tundra and ice deserts of the 15,000-foot-high Tibetan plateau, where the remoteness of this region and Chinese law afford the animals at least some protection.

Kashmir Stag (India)
Also known as the hangul, this deer once was considered the property of the Maharajah of Kashmir, who protected it. Ever since India took possession of Kashmir in 1947, enforcement has not been adequate to keep poachers and shepherds from invading the hangul's mountainous sanctuaries.

Golden Takin (China)
Only four and one half feet high, the golden takin is a stocky beast weighing 600 pounds. This rare, bulbous-nosed animal lives high on the Great White Mountain in central China; there it dines on bamboo shoots amid rhododendron near the timber line.

Key Deer (Florida)
Nibbling in a palmetto thicket, this tiny deer is more likely to be killed by an automobile than by a bullet. Hunting has been controlled effectively, but its once large and wild habitat in Florida's Keys is now resort country overcrowded with tourists and their cars.

Tule Elk (California)
Hungry gold prospectors almost wiped out the tule elk in the 1840s; by 1885 there were only 28. Since then, they have increased to 485, largely because of the protection provided by three reserves in California's chaparral region.

Giant Sable Antelope (Angola)
Two males lock the majestic five-foot horns so desired by trophy-seekers. Though Angola created two reserves to shelter the few remaining herds of this antelope, native trappers will, for a price, supply an armchair hunter with horns, head or hide to decorate his den.

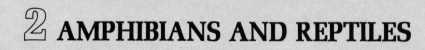 2 AMPHIBIANS AND REPTILES

In the earth's dim past, life first emerged as shapeless blobs in primeval seas. The earliest vertebrates were fishes, whose perpetuation was entirely dependent on surrounding waters. But there came a time when rising land masses stranded many of these creatures. Their survival became dependent on the ability to venture ashore. Those that made the transition were the first amphibians, and they did it by developing an air-breathing anatomy and fins adapted for moving on land. However, amphibians still had to remain as close as possible to water because their pattern of reproduction demanded it.

The major evolutionary breakthrough was accomplished by reptiles, the first creatures to lay hard-shelled eggs, thereby endowing their embryos with a portable watery environment. Thereafter, it was possible for an animal to spend its entire life cycle on land—an advantage later inherited by mammals and birds. In fact, the familiar question "Which came first, the chicken or the egg?" would seem to be answered in favor of the egg. Nevertheless, many reptiles were unable to resist an ancestral yearning for water: alligators, crocodiles, some snakes and some turtles now lead a mainly aquatic life, although they must surface to breathe and most return to land to lay their eggs.

Compared to most of the world's birds and mammals, there is little in the appearance and behavior of amphibians and reptiles to win them the impulsive affection of humans. Slithery, scaly, cold-blooded and sometimes venomous, these relics of an ancient age have long figured in mankind's legends, myths and religions either as symbols of evil or as objects of reverent awe. In Greek lore, Medusa's headful of writhing snakes supposedly transformed the beholder to stone; in Teutonic mythology, the serpent Nidhögg perpetually gnawed at the roots of the giant ash tree that represented the world; and in medieval tales, heroic knights were forever slaying fire-breathing dragons.

The few dragons left are the so-called Komodo dragons—the monitor lizards that inhabit a few remote Indonesian islands. They do not breathe fire, and even in the absence of errant knights, they are very much endangered. So are many of their reptile brothers and amphibian cousins. Throughout the world men are chopping down their forests, polluting their streams, draining their swamp retreats and killing them for their hides or for their usually tasty flesh. As a rule, they receive little in the way of legislative protection. There have been few sentimental pleas on their behalf, but they nonetheless constitute a large and important segment of the ecological chain that links the entire animal world, including ourselves. For that reason alone, it is imperative to save these threatened species.

Frogs and Salamanders

Croaking frogs, slithering salamanders, warty toads —all vestiges of an ancient, pre-reptilian world— have for centuries played a central role in man's fears and superstitions. In Elizabethan England, frogs and a kind of salamander called a newt were thought to be basic ingredients of the brews made by witches; and in fairy tales toads are a symbol of ugliness. Perhaps that helps to explain why man has been largely indifferent to the plight of these truly harmless creatures.

Frogs and toads (which zoologists classify together) and salamanders are amphibians; they require water to carry out key phases of their life cycles. Although most species are essentially land dwellers, they breed and lay their eggs in or near ponds or streams. Their offspring, born with the gills of a fish, must spend their tadpole life under water until they metamorphose into air-breathing adults. This pattern means, of course, that none of them can stray far from the ancestral water hole.

Nature, which saddled them with this restriction, imposed yet another problem as the drying up of the earth's climates progressed and deserts began to form. Many species became stranded in small oases in the midst of arid territory. Not unexpectedly, the state of California, studded as it is with deserts, is host to a considerable number of rare and endangered amphibians.

Furthermore, California is leading the world in protecting these often-despised creatures—by forbidding their capture and by raising funds to buy parcels of the land on which they have managed to survive. Other states and countries, unfortunately, have been far less provident. Frogs, toads and salamanders usually are small enough to be captured easily, so collecting has been allowed to proceed unchecked—whether by little boys who catch the wriggly creatures merely for fun or by scientists who pickle the specimens in formaldehyde for future use in their laboratories.

Unless stringent protective measures are rigidly enforced, classroom editions of *Macbeth* may someday require a footnote explaining what Shakespeare meant by "Eye of newt, and toe of frog."

Panamanian Golden Frog (Panama)
This spectacular species is found only in a three-square-mile area of Panama called El Valle de Antón. The animal's bright color, reminiscent of the ornamental images of pre-Columbian times, is particularly attractive to tourists, who buy the golden frogs for pets. In defiance of Panamanian law, the frogs also have been shipped by the hundreds to collectors abroad.

Santa Cruz Long-toed Salamander (U.S.)
This five-inch variety breeds exclusively in two mud ponds of Santa Cruz County, California. Both of the ponds are small enough that they could be drained in a single day and both lie in areas coveted by land developers. The salamanders won a reprieve from almost certain extinction when the state, in 1973, bought the acreage surrounding one of the ponds for the express purpose of saving these rare creatures.

Pine Barrens Tree Frog (U.S.)
Smaller than a man's thumb, these tiny amphibians live in swampy areas of North Carolina and southern New Jersey. The adults generally are reclusive, but during the mating season males boast their presence with twangy calls.

Texas Blind Salamander (U.S.)
One of the rarest of American salamanders, this species lives in the total darkness of Purgatory Creek, deep in the eerie world of Ezell's Cave near San Marcos, Texas. Although the young are born with sight, their eyes atrophy from disuse. Unlike most amphibians, blind salamanders keep gills for breathing throughout their lives.

Slender Salamanders (U.S.)

Wormlike and thin-legged, slender salamanders are peculiar to the Pacific Coast. The Tehachapi variety (far left) and its closest relative, the Kern Canyon salamander (left), inhabit adjacent areas of Kern County, California.

Limestone Salamander (U.S.)

This tiny salamander would fit in the palm of a man's hand with some room to spare. Yet another of California's rare amphibians, it lives in crevices among moss-covered rocky slopes in only two square miles of limestone outcroppings in Mariposa County.

Chinese Giant Salamander (China)

By far the largest amphibian, this aquatic five-footer of the western Pacific is a great scavenger: almost any small swimming creature is a potential meal. That voracious appetite contributes to the giant salamander's endangerment; it eagerly snaps up the meat bait tendered by Chinese fishermen, who consider its flesh a delicacy.

Black Toad (U.S.)
A scant 12 acres of land near Death Valley, California, is the only remaining home for this midget subspecies of the common western toad. Countless black-toad tadpoles have perished as a result of drainage and canalization of their breeding streams.

Sonoran Green Toad (North America)
A network of dark lines surrounding yellow-green spots provides a natural camouflage for this rarely seen species, which ranges from southwestern Arizona to Sonora, in Mexico. The habitat of the Arizona colony is not threatened by civilization because it lies entirely within the Papago Indian Reservation. But there, as elsewhere, the green toads are significantly depleted by persistent collecting.

Turtles

Man is on the verge of annihilating the very animal that is the symbol of longevity. The turtle, clumsy and lumbering, has been venerated throughout mythology as a Methuselah among beasts. It is an amazingly long-lived reptile that epitomizes good health and durability—so much so that artists have depicted it sturdily supporting the globe.

Certain turtles can, in fact, live for more than a century, and they will tenaciously tolerate an incredible amount of injury. Such endurance has helped them persist, relatively unchanged, for almost 200 million years. This ancient lineage is borne as much by two-inch-long children's pets as by rare monsters that measure nine feet between flipper-tips and weigh nearly a ton.

Vulnerably slow moving on land, most turtles prefer an aquatic life: land-bound turtles (usually called tortoises) often seek marshy ponds, while sea turtles require the salty ocean that buoys their bulk. In fact, their weight nearly crushes their lungs when they crawl ashore. Yet crawl they must, at least once a year, because their ancestors evolved on land: turtle eggs will not hatch in water, so they must be laid in pits in the soil. This evolutionary bind is one cause of turtles' present peril. Although the females often lay up to 200 eggs at a time, these nutritious delicacies are snatched up by turtle hunters, who also snare the ponderous parents when they rise for air from submarine feeding grounds.

Hunters sell turtles for their oil, skins, shells and flesh. Once extolled as antidotes for scurvy and as elixirs of life, turtle meat and soup are today delights for the gourmet. To add to the turtles' plight, new resorts are obliterating many nesting beaches, and thirsty housing developments are lowering the water tables in turtle ponds.

To stem the rapid depletion of major species, some local governments, notably that of Queensland in Australia, have banned the capture of turtles. Others are creating turtle preserves, licensing turtle hunting at sea, banning the sale of turtle products and raising hatchlings on turtle farms. But several governments continue to do nothing at all, preferring to profit handsomely from turtle sales.

Radiated Tortoise
Only about 18 inches long, these rare 15-pound vegetarians are among the most beautiful and most valuable of turtles. Tribesmen of their native Madagascar consider them magical and leave them alone, but the Malagasy government allows radiated tortoises to be exported for a fee, and collectors are more than willing to pay upwards of $300 for a single specimen.

Hawksbill Turtle

The hawksbill, which uses its hooked beak to snip seaweed and extract mollusks from shells, once abounded in the warm parts of most of the world's oceans. But it is now the rarest and most threatened of turtles: its shell is prized by jewelers, and young specimens are mounted as curios.

Green Turtle

This brown, shallow-water seagrass grazer is named for the color of its fat. Its tender meat makes the green turtle the tastiest of turtles. Too often its shell lining becomes turtle soup, its oil goes into the manufacture of cosmetics and its skin becomes modish shoes.

Loggerhead Turtle

Sea turtles have bigger heads than land turtles, and the loggerhead's is especially large. In search of eelgrass, sponges, shellfish and jellyfish, it wanders thousands of miles. But its main nesting beaches are in Australia and South Africa—where protection exists —and the Atlantic Coast of the U.S., where the menace to its survival is a boom in housing construction.

Pacific Ridley Turtle
Olive-colored and smallest of the sea turtles, the ridley is most frequently found eating seaweed and mollusks at the bottom of a shallow bay. The female migrates to the same beach each year to lay her eggs in a hole dug above the high-tide line. The hatchlings instinctively crawl downhill toward the surf. Only a small per cent of the young survive human and animal predators.

Leatherback Turtle
The largest of all turtles, these three-quarter-ton reptiles have five-foot-long shells that consist of leathery skin instead of horny plates. Unlike other sea turtles, whose forelimbs are modified into small flippers, they have paddle-shaped appendages. One of their principal rookeries is in Malaysia, where egg gatherers strip the beach clean, selling the eggs for 17 cents each.

Galápagos Giant Tortoise
In Spanish, tortoises are called galápagos, the name given the Pacific
archipelago by 16th Century explorers.
Over the years whalers tied thousands
of these 500-pound reptiles on their
decks to provide fresh meat. Rats and
domestic animals introduced by settlers still devour the eggs and young.
These harmless vegetarians sleep 16
hours a day, keep cool with mud baths
and let finches clean them of ticks.
Breeding stations subsidized by Ecuador and UNESCO are now protecting most of the remaining rookeries.

Crocodiles and Alligators

Crocodilians are divided into three families: crocodiles; alligators and caimans, with broader, more rounded snouts than crocodiles'; and gavials, with long, tapering muzzles. They vary in size from three-foot dwarfs to 25-foot monsters. The last surviving reptilian descendants of the creatures that gave rise to dinosaurs, the crocodilians have thrived unchallenged for 140 million years. They originated as land dwellers and then returned to the water. Most now live in rivers, marshes and deltas in the world's temperate and tropic regions. Although they usually stay within a relatively small area, some have been known to swim hundreds of miles.

It is a discouraging truth about these reptiles that conservationists have difficulty arousing much sympathy for them. In the popular mind, the gaping jaws of alligators and crocodiles, and their widely accepted reputations as voracious man-eaters, relegate them to the category of pests, suited only to supply the handsome, durable skins that are used for elegant leather accessories.

But some alligators and crocodiles cannot even claim valuable hides. Johnston's crocodile in Australia, for example, has an inferior skin that wears poorly, yet local poachers seldom are particular; they trap whatever specimens they can find for whatever price they can command. Nonetheless, the fact is that crocodiles and alligators, like snakes, most often are killed simply out of fear.

Only a few of these reptiles actually are man-eaters—or woman-eaters, a special characteristic of Nile crocodiles, which have made occasional meals of East African women incautiously washing their clothes at the river's edge. The reputation of Asia's estuarine crocodiles also suffers from their sporadic attacks on people.

Unfortunately the worldwide demand for apparel made with crocodile and alligator skins has outlasted the onetime fads for elaborate plumes and exotic furs, and governments have been reluctant to discourage the clothing industry by legislative means. Where protective legislation exists it tends to be poorly enforced—or circumvented relatively easily by nocturnal poachers.

Johnston's Crocodile (Australia)
Small, shy and harmless to man, this narrow-jawed crocodile eats almost anything—turtles, water rats, frogs, fish and insects. Although the species receives protection in Western Australia and the Northern Territory, poachers come from Queensland to snare hatchlings for tourist trophies.

Estuarine Crocodile (Asia, Australia)
A resident of tidal rivers, mangrove swamps and river deltas, this rare saltwater reptile has been known to grow to a length of 25 feet. In New Guinea the skin of the species is a prime source of income, so plans were devised for a hatchery that would simultaneously allow the wild-crocodile population to recover and produce enough skins for a profitable local tannery.

Nile Crocodile (Africa)
Described by Herodotus and venerated by the crocodile cults of African tribes, this large reptile was once widespread in Africa. Today only a small number of males and nesting females remain in Uganda's Murchison Falls National Park. Poachers still skin several specimens a month and tourist boats disturb females guarding their eggs, thus allowing predators to move in.

American Alligator (United States)
Swamps, lakes and bayous on the Atlantic and Gulf coasts are home to this blunt-nosed, relatively harmless reptile. In winter it dozes in deep water holes that shelter marsh life, but Florida's canals and communities are draining the marshes. Nearly eliminated by poachers, this variety is beginning a comeback because of new legislation.

Yacaré Caiman (South America)
Rare eight-foot-long Yacaré caimans feast on snails, crabs, snakes and fish. Although closely related to alligators, caimans are more agile and have sharper teeth. Adults have bony plates on their bellies and backs, making their skins commercially useless, so hunters slaughter the plateless young instead.

Chinese Alligator (China)

The six-foot Yangtze Delta species is one of only two crocodilians in temperate latitudes. It is used by the Chinese for food, leather and medicine and may even have inspired their concept of a dragon. Winter finds it virtually hibernating in underground tunnels.

Gavial (Southeast Asia)

The gavial's narrow, beaklike jaws and long, thin teeth are adapted for catching fish. It is the most aquatic of all crocodilians. Lurking in rivers in India and Burma, the gavial faces extinction from hide collectors.

Spectacled Caiman (South America)

Named for a horny ridge connecting its eye sockets, this caiman feeds on giant snails and the fearsome piranha. Hidehunters have wiped out the adults near the Atlantic, and they are now pursuing them in inland rivers.

Tuataras

About 250 million years ago, long before the great dinosaurs, relatives of tuataras roamed the world. Both the tuataras and the dinosaurs subsequently appeared, but the dinosaurs reached gigantic proportions and vanished, leaving only fossil traces. Tuataras alone have survived, almost unchanged. They may even be the only link between ancient reptiles and modern lizards and snakes.

Very little is known about the intervening history of these enduring creatures. As a matter of fact, there are no known fossils from any part of the Tertiary period—from 2 million to 70 million years ago. In modern times, their world shrank gradually to the confines of the New Zealand archipelago and finally to some 20 remote islets off the coast of New Zealand's two main islands. Over that long time span, tuataras acquired odd physical attributes, including a third eye that remains in vestigial form at the top of the head.

Tuataras' remarkably slow evolution is more than matched by their astonishingly protracted life cycle: eggs are laid about 10 months after fertilization and take 15 months or so to hatch; the young do not reach sexual maturity until they are 20 years old, and adults may live to be 100.

In their small island retreats, these harmless reptiles have a symbiotic relationship with shearwaters —local shore birds—and share their burrows. Low trees and shrubs in the region not only shade the numerous burrows but also harbor the insects that are the tuataras' main diet. Tuataras have disappeared from the islands where imported goats and sheep were allowed to multiply—these grazing animals quickly denuded the trees and thus eliminated the insect supply. The tuataras that did not starve were finished off by cats, dogs, rats and wild pigs.

As long as goats and predators are kept off their islands, these living fossils have a sporting chance. Mindful of these conditions, New Zealand authorities have introduced extremely strict regulations: no one is allowed on the offshore islands without a permit, severe penalties are imposed in cases of unauthorized capture, and extreme vigilance is exercised against the inadvertent arrival of cats and rats.

Tuatara (New Zealand)
This primitive lizard-like creature is a member of a relict reptilian order. Its rather fearsome appearance belies its size; the adult male is only two feet long, including its tail, and seldom weighs more than two pounds.

Lizards

A litter of kittens is accidentally left ashore by a merchant ship island-hopping across the Pacific. A sere California valley is transfigured into a fertile agricultural oasis as engineers complete an irrigation project. Predatory mongooses are deliberately introduced to Fiji to protect the sugar-cane plantations from snakes. These seemingly unrelated events have in common a single theme—they represent critical threats to several of the more than 3,000 species of lizards.

When kittens—which can grow into wild cats—and mongooses are transferred to new environments, they become predators. Then, lacking natural enemies, they breed unchecked. And when land is cleared, whether for needed farmland or for a new retirement community, forage and shelter are destroyed for many species, including lizards.

It is ironical that lizards are being jeopardized in this indirect fashion; throughout history these descendants of dinosaurs have had little direct contact with humans, since the regions they inhabit have in the past been far removed from the paths of developing civilizations.

But now some lizard species are under extreme pressure, particularly the ones found on Pacific and Caribbean islands and in the deserts of northern Mexico and the southwestern United States. Though geographically disparate, these areas are similar in that the affected lizards—try as they may to move from man's advance—have few available retreats.

In most of these localities, the vanishing species are nominally protected by law, but the indirect problems stemming from introduction of exotic animals and from habitat destruction so far have proved impossible to regulate. California has proposed the establishment of a section of the San Joaquín Valley—the home of several endangered lizard species—as a haven for sample specimens of all of the region's flora and fauna.

Since most lizards survive but do not breed in captivity, it is only by creating or preserving such stabilized habitats—by maintaining natural cycles of predation and natural pockets of shelter—that the lizards of the world can be saved.

Marine Iguana (Galápagos Islands)
An inhabitant of the rocky shorelines of the Pacific islands some 650 miles off the coast of Ecuador, the marine iguana is the only living lizard that has an aquatic habitat. It dives into the water for its food—seaweed—and uses the ocean as a convenient escape route from hungry wild dogs, cats or rats.

San Diego Horned Lizard (U.S.)
Once common in Southern California, this lizard—often called the horned toad because of its spine-studded hide —thrives in dry brushland. But little of its habitat is left since the region has become one of the fastest-developing areas in the United States.

Black Legless Lizard (U.S.)
Sleek, slender and snakelike, this eight-inch reptile belongs to a small family of lizards with no trace of leg development. It prefers moist, sandy areas along a limited stretch of California's coastline and is perhaps the most critically endangered of all lizards.

Reticulate Gila Monster (U.S., Mexico)
*Flicking its scent-perceptive tongue, a
two-foot-long Gila tracks a prospective
victim through the desert. One of only
two types of venomous lizards, it has a
bite that is painful and debilitating but
usually not fatal to man.*

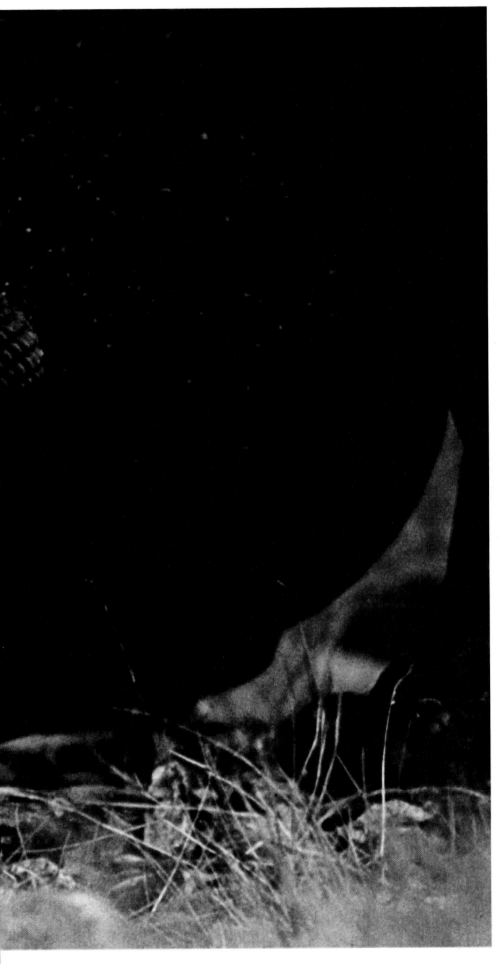

Komodo Island Monitor (Indonesia)
This giant reptile measures almost 10 feet in length and weighs some 200 pounds. It is usually called the Komodo dragon after its native Indonesian island—and a presumed resemblance to mythological dragons. It feeds on an ever-dwindling supply of wild pigs, deer and carrion. In extreme cases it has been known to attack—and bring down—a half-ton water buffalo.

177

Blunt-nosed Leopard Lizard (U.S.)
The bright red spots of a female advertise her approaching motherhood; after her eggs are laid, the blotches will disappear. Hopes for the survival of this species grow ever more tenuous as irrigation engineers continue to turn California's once-arid San Joaquín Valley into lush farmland.

Galápagos Land Iguana (Galápagos)
Although Charles Darwin found so many land-iguana burrows on a single island that he had to tread cautiously, there now are only a few hundred of the lizards in the entire archipelago. The outlook for future generations is precarious: the islands' protective underbrush is being eaten away by goats, thereby exposing the young lizards to sharp-eyed birds of prey.

Fiji Banded Iguana (Fiji, Tonga Islands)
As her bright hue suggests, this female frequents dense tropical vegetation—a milieu vanishing before the impact of a tourist-oriented real-estate boom. The male of this tree-dwelling species is equally well camouflaged by stripes of gray and green, but protective coloration has been of little help in avoiding the islands' mongooses.

Rhinoceros Iguana (West Indies)
One of the lizards still hunted for food, the primitive rhinoceros iguana—so called for the hornlike spurs above its nostrils—is imperiled in such heavily populated Caribbean areas as Haiti and the Dominican Republic.

Snakes

Among Western peoples the serpent is the very symbol of evil, but there are other cultures that treat snakes with reverence and awe. Several West African tribes decree death for anyone who kills a python, their god of wisdom, and devout Hindus set out bowls of milk every night to placate the cobra, which is regarded as a household deity. Throughout India the cobra is depicted around temple doorways—it is the symbolic protector that safeguards the treasures within.

Snakes have existed for at least 100 million years, adapting themselves to deserts, forests, swamps, prairies, salty seas. Everywhere they have fulfilled an important function—controlling the populations of insects, lizards, mammals, birds, fish. Wherever they disappear, the ecological balance is thrown out of kilter. Yet apprehension and hatred are their greatest enemies.

Actually, the physical characteristics that inspire such fear and loathing generally are harmless to man. The flickering tongue that some people falsely believe to be venomous serves only to help a snake sample food or track its prey: it picks up any particles it finds and carries them to an olfactory organ located in the roof of its mouth. The venomous teeth borne by a minority of snakes make people fear the bite of all snakes, though most species deliver nothing worse than a pinch. Size has relatively little to do with a snake's harmfulness but it is rather difficult to dispute the argument that 10 yards of anaconda is always heart-fluttering.

Given the chance, all snakes will avoid a showdown with an enemy, but the belief persists that they are aggressive and that the only good snake is a dead snake. Snakes have been slaughtered indiscriminately both for their skins and for their rather tasty flesh, and also because they have been known to raid barnyards and chicken houses, but in the end they are killed principally because most people are irrationally afraid of them.

Since legal protection for snakes is practically nonexistent throughout the world, there is an urgent need to recognize the fact that these creatures are far more to be valued than despised.

Madagascar Boa (Madagascar)
Equally at home in rivers or forests, this rare nine-foot snake is prized by local hunters. Zoos—particularly in the United States and Western Europe—pay excessive prices for a single specimen. Since this boa has an unusually low reproduction rate, it is difficult for the species to compensate for the many losses it sustains.

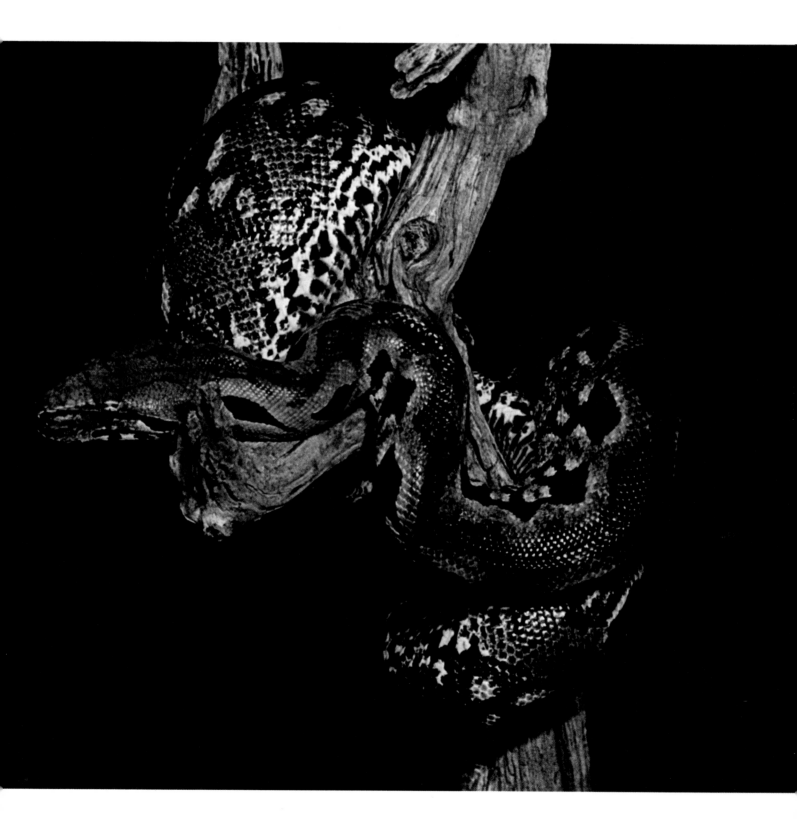

Arizona Ridge-nosed Rattlesnake (U.S.)
Millions of years ago the American Southwest, covered with forests, grew warmer and drier. The desert took over and the woodlands shrank to mountain-top pockets. The ridge-nosed rattler, a forest denizen, survived the transition but now has a limited range.

Alameda Striped Racer (California)
Rustling through the dry brush and gullies in the foothills near San Francisco Bay, this orange-bellied snake preys on lizards, birds and other snakes. But the region has sprouted bedroom communities for San Francisco, and there is little room for racers.

Indian Python (South Asia)
The female Indian python lays about
100 eggs at a time and broods them like
a hen, pushing all the eggs into a pile
and coiling her body around them. Despite such prodigious numbers of offspring, the species is fast disappearing.
Hide-hunters manage to swallow their
fear of this 20-foot, 200-pound python,
since bags and wallets made of its bold-
ly patterned skin command high prices.

San Francisco Garter Snake (U.S.)
This colorful snake resides in bulrush-
es bordering lakes and ocean inlets in
the western half of San Francisco's
peninsula. Overgrown banks have been
cleared to improve the flow of water, and as a consequence, only a few
hundred of these snakes still survive.

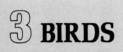 **BIRDS**

About 140 million years ago, long after the early mammals had appeared, a lizard-like creature acquired the ability to lift itself off the ground. *Archaeopteryx,* as paleontologists call this relative newcomer to the animal kingdom, had a reptilian face—complete with teeth—and three clawed fingers at the end of its wing bones. But it was feathered, and thus it shared the one characteristic common to all birds.

As the millennia rolled by, nature refined its latest invention and the bird species multiplied until there were some 11,600 different ones, all living at the same time. Eventually, the total slumped to the 8,500 or so species in existence today. In spite of this decrease, birds still outnumber all vertebrates, excluding fishes.

The sights and sounds of the world of birds are as varied as the species themselves. They include not only the majestic sweep of a bald eagle, the precise formation of migrating wild geese, the ominous hovering of vultures above a dying beast, but also the trill of a nightingale deep in the woods at night, the chatter of city sparrows at dawn, the happy cacophony of barnyard fowl, the call of sea gulls near shore and, perhaps most unforgettable, the flight of a lark soaring ever higher toward a boundless sky, all the while singing a song of exultation.

The gift of flight has mesmerized man since earliest times. His earthbound frustrations were mirrored in fantastic tales ranging from the Greek legend of Icarus, who used homemade wings of feathers and wax for an ill-fated flight to the sun, to the 19th Century novels of Jules Verne about trips to the moon. More practical men attempted to devise workable flying machines by studying the mechanics of bird flight. Ironically, the first successful flight of Orville and Wilbur Wright occurred just a few years after the most spectacular, complete disappearance of a wild-bird species. Once the most numerous bird in the world—with a population estimated at three to five billion in the early 1800s—passenger pigeons became extinct in less than a century. They had been gunned down and trapped in nets by the thousands, and most ended up as squab on the nation's dining tables.

Compared to the original staggering numbers of passenger pigeons, each bird species now consists of a mere handful. Many are on the decline; too many are still unprotected, and they could be wiped out in much less than a century. Too often, the soaring flight of a golden eagle ends in a burst of burned flesh on a high-tension wire and the dive of a cormorant leads it to drowning in an undersea lobster trap. Pesticides, which frequently find their way into the food supply of birds, cause infertility in many species. No longer do even the seas provide a safe haven: the oil from a single tanker disaster in 1967 killed 20,000 penguin-like murres in the English Channel.

Water Birds

In envy, man through the centuries has aspired to be "free as a bird." In fact, birds are more linked to their environs than humans; they cannot simply fly away from the pressures in their lives. Some water birds have extremely restricted habitats, limited in some instances to a single lake or island where the effects of any ecological disturbance are amplified. For example, pigs and dogs introduced into Hawaii by Western settlers preyed on the Hawaiian goose to the point of near-extinction. All the birds of the Galápagos Islands live today with the same potential threat. Similarly, plants introduced accidentally or intentionally can crowd out vegetation on which birds depend for food or cover.

Water birds that have only one nesting ground obviously are most vulnerable unless hunting is rigidly policed but those with wider ranges also are in peril. Wild ducks and geese make especially delicious meals, but then hungry sailors have never scorned albatross or penguin. And of course the eggs of all birds tend to find their way into omelets.

Nor is food the only motive for hunting. At the turn of the century, the American egret nearly disappeared because of the Victorian rage for feathered hats; other water birds such as the Laysan duck also have barely survived avid plume hunters.

Though it can be extremely difficult to protect habitats and control hunting, even more ominous is the problem of pollution. Most of the seas are now dotted with oil slicks. The unwary bird that lands on one finds its feathers so coated that it cannot fly, and it soon dies. In addition there are the invisible chemical agents. Conservationists suspect that Japanese crested ibis have become rare as a result of the mercury-based sprays used in the flooded rice fields where they feed. Even birds that live in remote or primitive areas are not safe from modern poisons, since the residues can be carried thousands of miles: the eggs of Cape Barren geese, whose habitat is Australia's coastal islands, have been found laden with pesticides. Were governments to act quickly and in concert to control the chemicals, years would pass before the damage would be undone: many pesticides are very long-lived.

Trumpeter Swan (North America)
In the 18th and 19th centuries multitudes of trumpeter swans — so named in tribute to their fanfare-like calls — were killed both for sport and for their down, which was made into powder puffs for European ladies. Nonetheless, the species probably has been saved from extinction by a vigorous 40-year-long conservation program. Most of the birds are now protected in Montana's Red Rock Lakes Refuge.

Cape Barren Goose (Australia)
A grass eater, this rare goose must compete for food with the huge sheep population imported to its native coastal islands. The species is fully protected by law, but stock grazers, who consider live geese as pests and dead ones as delicacies for their tables, nevertheless hunt the birds.

Laysan Duck (Hawaii)
Endemic to Laysan Island in the Hawaiian archipelago, this species nearly disappeared in the 19th Century when wild rabbits almost ate the island bare. With the rabbits exterminated and the island included in the Hawaiian Islands National Wildlife Refuge, a recently established captive-breeding program may add significant numbers to the current population of several hundred.

Waved Albatross (Galápagos)
Two albatrosses court on Hood Island, their only breeding ground. These oceanic nomads spend months out in the Pacific, sleeping on the waves, feeding on squid and small fish; they return to land only to mate and raise their young. The widespread superstition that killing an albatross brings years of bad luck protects these birds to some degree. But since the entire population gathers to nest on just one island, a single catastrophe, man-made or natural, could spell the end of the species.

Atitlán Grebe (Guatemala)
This flightless species is found only in volcano-ringed Lake Atitlán. Never abundant, the population began to tumble after 1957 when the lake was stocked with bass to attract sports fishermen. The voracious bass eat not only the small crabs and fish on which grebes feed, but grebe chicks as well. The endangered bird faces a worse threat: a hydroelectric plant is slated for the lake's shore. If it is built, the water level will drop, and the grebe's reedy nesting grounds will disappear.

Japanese Crested Ibis (Japan)
Deforestation throughout the Far East has deprived this beautiful bird of the tall trees it requires for nesting and roosting. Only a tiny flock of a dozen survives tenuously in a wooded sanctuary on Japan's Sado Island.

Hawaiian Goose (Hawaii)
Also called the nene, this bird leads an un-gooselike life around the dry lava fields of Hawaii's volcanoes. Almost extinguished in the wild by hunting, it breeds so well in captivity (left) that several hundred have been released to their native haunts. Though still relatively rare, there is a good chance that Hawaii's state bird will survive.

Dalmatian Pelican (Eurasia)
Among the largest flying birds, Dalmatian pelicans are dwindling rapidly in numbers. They nest in the Balkan countries but have been tracked during migrations as far away as Mongolia. Each year they return faithfully to eastern Europe, often finding their retreats eliminated and their prospects for undisturbed breeding diminished.

Flightless Cormorant (Galápagos)
This master swimmer walks awkwardly on land and is an easy mark for hunters. On the ocean bottom, where it feeds, many cormorants have been snared and drowned in lobster traps set by fishermen. Acquisitive zoos have also whittled down the flocks.

201

Eastern Brown Pelican (North America)
A pelican fledgling invades its mother's mouth for a fish, while its sibling nestles tranquilly nearby. Throughout the southeastern states, pesticides continue to claim victims: the chemicals contaminate fish on which the pelicans feed and cause the females to lay eggs too thin-shelled to hatch.

Galápagos Penguin (Galápagos Islands)
Mother and baby penguins bask under a tropical sun. The only penguins living at the equator, they fish in the cool Humboldt Current, which sweeps around the islands, and often encounter sharks, their natural enemy. On shore, egg collectors menace their nests.

Rheas

The largest bird in the New World, the rhea of South America is frequently called the American ostrich for its superficial resemblance to Africa's only flightless bird. Like the ostrich, the rhea has powerful legs with which to deliver fierce defensive kicks. These same limbs enable it to flee from danger at speeds approaching 40 miles per hour. Even at top speed, with its head and neck almost parallel to the ground, a rhea can make an abrupt and bewildering right-angle turn to throw off its enemies —wild dogs, pumas or men.

There are only two living species of rhea: Darwin's rhea (right) and the gray rhea. Both are imperiled by hunters and the advance of civilization. Although the rhea is protected by Argentine law, Indians and ranchers still track it through the grasslands, corralling whole flocks in enormous nets. The rhea's meat then becomes food for sheep dogs, its skin is made into a rug or wallets, its mottled feathers are turned into feather dusters, and each of its six toes becomes a good-luck charm. In the 19th Century about 500,000 rheas were killed each year merely for their feathers. Indians and gauchos chased them on horseback and hobbled them by hurling a stone-tipped thong known as a bola. Even today, rheas that stray onto public roads in Argentina are likely to be shot. In order to avoid such slaughter, a few conscientious ranchers have provided vast fenced enclosures where the birds can live unmolested.

Male rheas are champion baby-sitters. Each of the half dozen or so females constituting a male's harem lays a clutch of pale-green eggs in a communal nest, and from then on she is relieved of duty. The male takes charge and incubates as many as 60 eggs at a time over a span of five to six weeks. After that, he still acts as guardian and provides food for the brood of chicks until they are well able to fend for themselves.

In captivity, rheas are prolific breeders, and this ultimately may offer the best solution to the preservation of the species since there appears to be little hope that the inadequate protective laws that now exist will be enforced more rigidly.

Darwin's Rhea (South America)
First collected in Argentina during the 19th Century voyage of the Beagle, Darwin's rhea stands four to four and one half feet tall and weighs about 60 pounds. It is found in grasslands in the southern third of the continent down to Tierra del Fuego. A few isolated flocks live in dry, sheltered pockets of the Andes as far north as Bolivia.

Game Birds

Pheasants, bobwhites and prairie chickens are all heavy-bodied birds not much given to flying. Their sturdy claws are adapted to scratching the ground for appealing items—insects, worms, roots, seeds.

All of Asia's endangered pheasants are forest creatures, and the population explosion in that part of the world has shrunk their habitats as forests have been cut to make way for humans and to fulfill an increasing demand for wood. The bobwhites and prairie chickens of North America prefer wide-open spaces, but they have also been routed, primarily by farmers and stock grazers.

Game birds everywhere are sought for their meat, and pheasants have the added attraction of opulent plumage. Chinese and Japanese bird fanciers prize them as pets or display stuffed specimens among their *objets*. After the Japanese occupied Taiwan in 1895, they sent home quantities of pheasants—indeed, the species that was chosen to grace the Japanese emperor's palace grounds has come to be known as the Mikado pheasant. Zoos, too, have been guilty of reducing wild pheasants to a dangerously low level, and there still is a profitable trade in these birds, even though all species are now protected by national laws.

The Pheasant Trust in Great Witchingham, England, has succeeded in raising pheasants from Taiwan, and in 1967 a few were released in a forest reserve owned and protected by the National Taiwan University. Similar projects have been proposed for China's brown eared pheasant and the peacock pheasant of the Philippines. Masked bobwhites already have been bred at the Patuxent Wildlife Research Center in Maryland and then reintroduced into their former Arizona range.

Most game birds lay 5 to 15 eggs each year and multiply rapidly in captivity. There is always the danger, however, that inbreeding over several generations within a small captive population will bring out harmful recessive traits that are suppressed in more genetically diverse wild flocks. But there is no point in returning game birds—or any other pen-reared creatures—to a natural habitat where the only future that awaits them is extinction.

Mikado Pheasant (Taiwan)
This elegant pheasant was unknown to Westerners until 1906, when a British bird collector spotted two of its striking tail feathers adorning a hill native's headdress. Probably never prevalent, the bird lives in forests atop precipitous sandstone cliffs, where it searches for berries, ferns and grubs. The species is on the verge of extinction, but the mountain dwellers still snare as many as they can, knowing that the pheasant commands a handsome price either alive or dead.

Swinhoe's Pheasant (Taiwan)
This colorful bird, with flashy red legs and eye patches, has rarely been seen in its subtropical habitat. Since ornithologist Robert Swinhoe described the bird in 1862, only one other naturalist has braved the heat and abundance of leeches in Taiwan's central mountain region to study it in the wild.

Palawan Peacock Pheasant (East Asia)
A feathered jewel, this pheasant lives in the rain forests of the Philippine island of Palawan. Since World War II the plains and foothills have been stripped for farmland, and the pheasant population has waned. Even breeding is a slow business; the hens lay only about two eggs each year.

Brown Eared Pheasant (China)
Named for the curious earlike tuft of feathers on either side of its head, this rare pheasant lives in the pine- and birch-forested mountains of northeastern China. Because these birds ramble in flocks, they make easy catches for meat-poor peasants, who seem undeterred by the tough, stringy flesh.

Masked Bobwhite (Mexico)
The scrubby mesquite plains of north-western Mexico and southern Arizona once were covered with tall grasses, where these quail nested and fed. In the 19th Century cattle overgrazed and trampled the grass so thoroughly that it never grew back; by 1912 the birds had disappeared from Arizona. The Mexican state of Sonora now has the only remaining wild flocks.

Northern Greater Prairie Chicken (U.S.)
Prairie chickens fled before the plows of pioneers who had discovered the extraordinary fertility of the American prairie. The birds themselves briefly turned pioneers, settling the new grasslands that sprang up where 19th Century lumbermen felled forests. But their vast range—from Ohio to Colorado, Arkansas to Canada—has become perhaps the most intensively cultivated region of the continent. Several states, led by Wisconsin, have established reserves and banned hunting to save their remaining prairie chickens.

Cranes, Rails and Bustards

Although the whooping crane has become a symbol to Americans of all endangered wildlife, the less publicized plight of other birds in the order of Gruiformes is equally worthy of concern. It is an ancient group—nine-million-year-old bones are still indistinguishable from those of modern species—but indiscriminate human assaults threaten to obliterate species that have endured for eons.

Farmers in India have driven bustards from their grasslands and shot these heaviest of all flying birds for food and sport. The gun also has been the scourge of the long-legged cranes. In 1670 Father Marquette, the French missionary-explorer, wrote to his superior that the Illinois Indians enjoyed fine crane hunting. The white man put an end to that within two centuries. Canada and the U.S. tardily banned the shooting of all migratory cranes in 1916; by then, however, the whooping crane was virtually extinct. In 1964 both governments buckled under pressure from angry farmers who complained that the still-common lesser sandhill crane was feeding on their crops. Hunting that species once again became legal, and consequently the whooping crane is today in greater jeopardy: the two species migrate together. There are perhaps 80 whoopers left, and if even one is shot by a hunter who cannot tell the two species apart, it is a tragedy of large proportion.

Included among the rails is an odd bird, the takahé. About 70 million years ago the islands that now constitute New Zealand separated from Antarctica; as this land raft drifted north and east, no mammals except bats were aboard. Ancestors of the takahé, with no predatory mammals to flee, gradually lost the ability to fly. But predators eventually arrived with settlers who brought weasels, pigs and dogs—mortal enemies of defenseless ground birds. By 1900 the takahé was thought to be extinct, but in 1948 an ornithologist discovered a handful in a New Zealand valley so remote and wild that he may well have been the first human there. The government moved quickly to create an enormous reserve that includes what is now called Takahé Valley. If two-footed and four-footed hunters can be kept out, the tenacious takahé may yet survive.

Whooping Crane (North America)
The settling of Canada and the Plains States was a catastrophe for whooping cranes: the last nest was found in the United States in 1896, and today they breed only at Great Slave Lake in the northern Canadian wilderness. Each fall, game wardens at the Aransas National Wildlife Refuge in Texas, the crane's sole wintering spot, anxiously count the arriving birds. They are on their own during their epic 2,000-mile migration, and careless hunters and bad storms are a few of the obstacles they might encounter.

Japanese Crane (East Asia)
For centuries the striking plumage of these graceful birds has made them a favorite subject of Japanese and Chinese painters. But since the marshes they inhabited in China, Manchuria and Japan have been drained to provide land for human use, only a few wetlands are left to shelter the remaining birds. In 1935 the crane was declared a national monument in Japan.

Kagu (New Caledonia)

This flightless forest bird has retreated to the remote steep valleys of its Pacific island. Melanesians once trapped the kagu for its plumes, and 19th Century French colonizers sold its feathers to European hatmakers. The French also brought along dogs that became wild and now are the endangered bird's principal enemy. The kagu's weird, piercing yelp has been recorded and is used by the New Caledonian radio station to sign on and off each day.

Mississippi Sandhill Crane (U.S.)

Forty years ago this crane seemed to have disappeared from the U.S. Gulf Coast, but in 1938 fifty of the birds were discovered in a tiny corner of one Mississippi county. Since then their numbers have fallen off as the remaining marshes have been planted with pine trees and covered over by roads and suburbs. Sandhill cranes are being raised at the Patuxent Wildlife Research Center in Maryland with an eye to releasing them to the wild.

Takahé (New Zealand)
A single valley surrounded by ice-capped mountains is this flightless bird's last refuge. In that inaccessible region the takahé is reliant on snow grass, which it uses for food and for its tunnel-like nest. There are about 300 takahés in the valley, but they are notoriously slow breeders, so their numbers will never show a dramatic increase.

California Clapper Rail (U.S.)
The noisy clatter of these rails fills the salt marshes of San Francisco Bay. At low tide they poke about the mud flats for snails, fiddler crabs and other crustaceans. Pollution has cut down the rails' food supply, and they risk DDT poisoning from the tidbits they do find.

Great Indian Bustard (South Asia)
The ostrich-like bustard lives in open grasslands where it is always on the alert for intruders. During breeding season the male struts about conspicuously with his white neck pouch so inflated that it makes an already easy target even easier for scofflaw hunters.

Parrots, Doves and Pigeons

Parrots and parakeets flash gaudily through all the world's tropical forests. They probably evolved first in Australasia, and from there they eventually spread to all of the continents except Antarctica, and to countless islands as well.

For thousands of years people have made pets of parrots and their smaller relatives, parakeets. Pliny wrote in the First Century A.D. that Emperor Nero had many African parrots brought to Rome, where he kept them in splendid cages of silver and ivory. In the 20th Century, their beautiful plumage and amusing ability to mimic words have led to an extensive and highly profitable commerce. Although many countries now protect their native parrots, trading still goes on. Australia, for example, imposes heavy fines on anyone who traps the sweet-singing grass parakeets, but bird dealers persist in subsidizing the offenders.

Parrots and parakeets are, in the main, forest dwellers and they have declined in numbers as agriculture has gobbled up their land. Among the exceptions are grass parakeets, which are adapted to open country, but their habitats have been taken over for livestock grazing. The dangers the birds face do not end there. When Nero grew bored with his parrots, he ate them, and these birds remain a source of food in many parts of Africa and Asia.

Wild pigeons and doves have been found virtually everywhere in the world's tropical and temperate regions. And for nearly 5,000 years—at least since Egyptian times—they have been collected and tamed. There is no scientific distinction between them: the smaller members of the family usually are called doves. The largest of all pigeons are the turkey-sized crowned pigeons of New Guinea and nearby islands. Like parrots, both pigeons and doves are killed for their meat, and the more exotic ones end up in zoos.

Parrots, pigeons and doves all reproduce in captivity and they are frequently long-lived—parrots sometimes reach 80 years of age. Though capture always has been the bane of these birds, the future of many species may depend on the practice, since they are fast disappearing in the wild.

Puerto Rican Parrot (Puerto Rico)
Puerto Rico has only one remaining large tract of virgin forest, where perhaps a dozen of these parrots struggle to survive. The birds nest only in large old Colorado trees—scores of which were cut down in the 1940s to make charcoal—and feed on fruit trees several miles away. The lengthy absences of the parents allow rats and pearly-eyed thrashers to raid the nests and eat the eggs and chicks. A poisoning program is getting rid of the rats, but there is no effective control for the thrashers.

Thick-billed Parrot (Mexico)
No Mexican would covet this parrot for a pet or as food, since it has a nasty bite and its flesh is rather tasteless. But as lumbermen have felled the Sierra Madre's great pine forests, the birds have become perilously rare. In search of pine nuts, their main food, they sometimes forage as far as Arizona and New Mexico.

St. Vincent Parrot (West Indies)
The gun—as well as the ax—is this colorful parrot's foe. Most of the mountainous forests of St. Vincent, where it prefers to live, have been cleared; in response, the bird has learned to nest near sea level, which may have slowed its decline. But resilience will never protect it adequately from West Indians who relish parrot stew.

Bahamas Parrot (Bahamas)
Bahamian Indians of 2,000 years ago littered their caves with parrots' bones; contemporary islanders still consider this bird a special dish. Not many are left for the pot, however: the parrots have disappeared from everywhere except Grand Inagua Island, which now harbors fewer than 1,000.

Golden-shouldered Paradise Parakeet
These birds nest on termite mounds in Australia, where animals introduced by settlers menace parents and chicks.

Masked Parakeet (Fiji)
No law protects this black-faced bird when it leaves its evergreen forests to raid fruit trees of irate islanders.

Golden Conure (Brazil)
A bare ring around each eye identifies conures and macaws. The conure is rare even in the steamy Amazon forests, and few are in captivity.

Indigo Macaw (Brazil)
The Indigo macaw is more easily heard than seen. Its noisy screech carries a mile, but in the rain forest its colorful feathers provide perfect camouflage.

Splendid Parakeet (Australia)
This rainbow of a bird is aptly named. Australia's grass parakeets—a group that includes both the splendid and the golden-shouldered paradise parakeets —are stars in the bird fancier's aviary. By the time Australia outlawed trapping the birds, traders had already done their share toward making them rare in the Outback.

Seychelles Turtle Dove (Seychelles)
The Seychelles in the Indian Ocean
have an abundance of doves, but the
richly colored indigenous species are
now seldom seen. When they inter-
breed with the drab-colored doves that
have been introduced from Madagascar, the hybrid offspring look more like
their foreign parents.

Victoria Crowned Pigeon (New Guinea)
Gregarious parties of these rare lacy-
crested birds wander through tropical
forests and swamps, feeding on fallen
fruit. When a plume hunter shoots one
of the pigeons, the others fly up to
nearby low branches where they com-
plain raucously and can then be picked
off easily one by one.

Hornbills and Trogons

There are few groups in the realm of birds so esthetically disparate as hornbills and trogons. Hornbills, with their oversized beaks and grotesque heads, seem bizarre. Trogons, by contrast, are so strikingly beautiful that one variety goes by the name resplendent. Because of their unusual looks, however, both types of birds have always captured the superstitious fancies of ancient peoples and primitive tribes.

The hornbills of Southeast Asia have been endowed with supernatural powers by natives. In Borneo, the local variety is revered by warriors as a lucky omen; on the Asian mainland, the bony casque atop the hornbill's skull is used in powder form as an aphrodisiac.

During the days of Montezuma the Central American trogon, named the quetzal by the Aztec, was associated with the serpent-god Quetzalcoatl. As a result, the quetzal's feathers were woven into ceremonial garb, including the elaborate headdress presented to Cortés by Montezuma in 1519. Indians in the region still view their resplendent quetzal with reverence. In Guatemala, for example, it is the national bird—displayed both on the flag and on currency. The quetzal is considered a symbol of freedom because the bird allegedly does not survive in captivity.

Today, hornbills and trogons are beset by commercialism. Quetzal feathers like those that once adorned Montezuma's cloak now are hawked as tourist souvenirs. Museums compete for quetzal-feathered skins, which are so fragile they often tear and disintegrate before reaching their destination. The ivory-like skulls of some Far Eastern hornbills are carved into snuff bottles, belt buckles and earrings; those whose skulls are too soft to carve are cooked as a delicacy.

Because of the rarity of hornbills and trogons, nearly all the species are endangered or at least vulnerable. Hopefully the governments of countries where they are found will soon follow Guatemala's lead: the nation's authorities have granted strict protection to their country's beloved symbol, and no quetzal has been exported in well over a decade.

Great Indian Hornbill (Southeast Asia)
The hornbill is an omnivorous bird with intriguing nesting habits. The female incubates her eggs for several weeks in a tree hollow that has been walled off from predators with mud. Meanwhile, the male forages for food and nourishes his burgeoning family through a hole pecked in the sturdy barrier to the nest. The future of great hornbills is threatened because natives consider their flesh more delectable than that of pheasant or chicken.

Resplendent Quetzal (Central America)
The striking red-and-green plumage of this Costa Rican trogon is an increasingly rare sight. Despite protective laws, poachers can earn the equivalent of two weeks' wages by selling a single pair to a foreign zoo. Farmers are destroying the bird's last stronghold by setting forest fires to create arable land.

Perching Birds

A world without the song of a single bird would seem truly inconceivable, yet songbirds are relative newcomers to our planet. The passerine—or perching-bird—order, to which they belong, only evolved about 60 million years ago. But they have made impressive progress since then: there are more than 5,000 species of perching birds, including all of the songbirds and some birds that do not sing. In fact, perching birds constitute about 60 per cent of the world's bird species.

Ranging in size from the little wren to the big, ornate lyrebird, perching birds are land birds that are represented on every island and continent except Antarctica. Most are superb fliers, but a few are fleet-footed and not much good in the air. Although other birds perch, only the passerines have specialized four-toed feet that secure them so well that they can sleep even on a wire without falling off. These birds also use their feet dexterously to hold food while they pry, crack, hammer or tear it with their multipurpose bills.

Although passerines seldom get high marks for brilliant plumage, there are some exceptions among them: the South American cock-of-the-rock, for example, is a spectacular specimen once referred to as "a fiery comet." Needless to say, it is a frequent target of plume hunters. Halfway around the world, in Indonesia, the Rothschild's starling (right) is also captured for its luxuriant plumage. But its popularity—and thus its decline—is the outcome of the excessive demands of the zoo and house-pet trade. Other perching birds that are talented mimics or melodious singers have succumbed to the same traffic.

Among the most endangered passerines, however, are those with narrow, restrictive habitats. The islands of Bali, Laysan and St. Kilda, for example, harbor distinctive species so limited in range that they are prime prospects for extinction. Islands —especially remote ones—have always been perilous places for avian life. Whether accidental or deliberate, the introduction of exotic species into those locations has eliminated endemic species and deprived the world of countless creatures, with perching birds ranking high on the mortality list.

Rothschild's Starling (Indonesia)
The creamy white feathers of these exquisite creatures are so slick and so seldom ruffled that the birds resemble porcelain figures. Slightly larger than common starlings, they have steel-blue eye patches and black wingtips. During courtship, the males and females sit and bob their heads toward each other and flourish their crests. The starlings live only in a small area of northern Bali, where the Bali-Barat reserve provides their only protection.

Rufous Scrub-Bird (Australia)
The forest habitat of this reddish-brown insect eater has been so reduced by years of drought and construction that it is found only in Lamington National Park near Brisbane. It spends most of its time on the ground.

White-necked Rock Fowl (West Africa)
Uncontrolled trapping for sales to museums, zoos and pet shops may quite soon extinguish this spectacular bald crow. It lives in forests among boulders, to which it plasters cup-shaped, grass-lined mud nests.

St. Kilda Wren (Outer Hebrides)
Only a few hundred of these sweet-voiced wrens inhabit 2,000 acres of the wild and remote St. Kilda archipelago. Although the birds are reasonably secure behind forbidding cliffs, a single intrusion, human or otherwise, could wipe out the entire population.

Laysan Finch (Hawaii)
This saucy, sparrow-sized songbird is
a rare descendant of continental American birds blown across the Pacific to
Hawaii. Native only to Laysan Island,
it is omnivorous, with a thick, hooked
bill for cracking other birds' eggs. The
finch also eats insects and carrion, and
even combs beaches for water-borne
pickings. Such opportunism saved it
from near-extinction when settlers introduced rabbits that ran wild and
destroyed much of the vegetation.

Cock-of-the-Rock (South America)
With a bright-orange crest that de-
scends low over its beak, a male cock-
of-the-rock is one of the most dazzling
birds in the Amazon rain forest. Males
live in clans separated from the dull-
brown females, but they establish special breeding areas. Brazilian tribesmen
fashion ceremonial headgear from the
males' feathers, but the increase in
farm acreage probably has had a greater impact on the population.

Birds of Prey

Because they are killers of living creatures as well as scavengers of the dead, birds of prey have inspired fear and revulsion for centuries. Yet through all this time they have survived man's vindictiveness—until recently. With the advance of technology, humans have become more adept at exacting revenge. Often it is an accidental reprisal through pesticides: as the birds feed they assimilate lethal concentrations of chemicals.

Although new laws have restricted the use of pesticides, the stubborn, lingering effects have persisted. DDT, for example, causes a hormonal imbalance; scientists first detected it among peregrine falcons, which started to produce eggs with shells too thin to survive the four-week incubation period. Other pesticides have rendered birds of prey infertile; this is particularly true of the bald eagle.

Nonetheless, the plague of poisons still takes second place to the losses inflicted by deliberate human assaults. Illegal attacks on protected birds and their nests continue, and existing laws are difficult to enforce; there is too much territory to cover and too few persons to do the work.

A number of significant steps are indeed being taken to safeguard the world's birds of prey, but the efforts are often limited or partly undermined. A few dozen California condors, for example, are sheltered in the 53,000-acre Sespe Condor Sanctuary, northwest of Los Angeles, which was established in 1951. Some incursions, however, are still allowed. The United States Forest Service issues permits for oil-drilling operations within the refuge, thereby encouraging intrusion on nesting birds that are highly sensitive to noise. And while the government of the Philippines has banned the capture of its few remaining monkey-eating eagles, as long as trophy collectors subsidize poachers, this eagle will be doomed to extinction.

Scattered pioneering studies to save endangered species are now underway. For example, at Cornell University resident scientists have artificially inseminated female hawks and falcons, thus attempting to redress in captivity the damage already done to these proud creatures in the wild.

African Lammergeyer (Africa, Arabia)
The lammergeyer's normal diet is restricted to carrion, but its reputation suffers from occasional rumors that one of these vultures has carried off a human baby. No such report has ever been confirmed, but the lammergeyer nonetheless has been a frequent victim of poisoning campaigns.

Peregrine Falcon (North America)
Peregrines have always been favored by devotees of the ancient sport of falconry, and illegal raids to capture prime specimens still claim a number of peregrine nestlings each year. But it is agricultural pesticides that have taken the largest toll.

Seychelles Kestrel (Seychelles)
Once familiar throughout its remote Indian Ocean habitat, the kestrel is now found only on the main island of Mahé, where it frequents populated areas and often falls victim to youngsters' slingshots. Its other enemy is the barn owl, which has usurped kestrel nesting sites, thus threatening to reduce still further a minuscule population.

Spanish Imperial Eagle (Spain)
This handsome nesting eagle probably is Europe's most critically endangered bird. Although it hunts only small game or steals food from other predators, suspicious Iberian chicken farmers regard it as a hated pest. The principal breeding area is in the Coto Doñana, a reserve in southwestern Spain.

Andean Condor (South America)
Soaring over the Pacific off Peru, a lone Andean condor epitomizes the species' majestic grace. This predator measures 10 feet between its wingtips and cruises effortlessly at speeds up to 80 miles an hour. An object of worship for hundreds of years, the condor is the national symbol of several Andean countries. But amateur hunters, who get 30 cents per feather and as much as $25 for an entire bird, have greatly reduced the condor population.

Everglade Kite (Florida)
This bird is also called the snail kite because its diet is limited to apple snails —its beak is specially adapted for spearing them in their shells. Draining of Everglades fresh-water marshes for agriculture and recreation has forced the snails to retreat to scattered parts of southern Florida. The population of kites, their diet and habitation thus restricted, is down below 100.

Southern Bald Eagle (North America)
Fully protected by federal law since 1940, the American national symbol has nonetheless been hurt primarily by the spread of insecticides and also deprived of many of its Florida nesting grounds by human encroachment. This bird's seven-foot wingspan and classic head have also made it a prime target of trophy collectors. There probably are fewer than 800 of these eagles left.

Monkey-eating Eagle (Philippines)
Demand for the monkey-eating eagle (right) as a stuffed trophy in Philippine homes has been the greatest cause of its decline. Even in its native habitat it reproduces very slowly, and attempts at breeding have thus far been futile. It is now almost extinct.

Galápagos Hawk (Galápagos Islands)
This young buzzard uses its talons to snare iguanas, snakes and chickens. In the past 50 years enraged chicken farmers have destroyed so many of the once-common birds that there now are fewer than 200 scattered throughout the Pacific archipelago.

California Condor (U.S.)
The California condor's days have been numbered ever since 19th Century prospectors began hunting it and driving it into remote mountain eyries. Sharpshooters and egg collectors have claimed countless victims since then; perhaps only 50 are left.

APPENDIX

International List of Endangered Animals

Below is a list of the world's animals that are currently in danger of becoming extinct. This information has been compiled from the International Union for Conservation of Nature and Natural Resources (IUCN), Morges, Switzerland; the United States Department of the Interior's Bureau of Sport Fisheries and Wildlife; and the 1973 Convention of International Trade in Endangered Species of Wild Life and Flora.

MAMMALS

Marsupialia
Macropus giganteus, Eastern gray kangaroo
Macropus giganteus tasmaniensis, Tasmanian forester kangaroo
Macropus fuliginosus, Western gray kangaroo
Megaleia rufa, Red kangaroo
Macropus parma, White-fronted wallaby or Parma wallaby
Setonix brachyurus, Quokka
Onychogalea frenata, Bridled nail-tail wallaby
Onychogalea lunata, Crescent nail-tail wallaby
Lagorchestes hirsutus, Western hare wallaby
Lagostrophus fasciatus, Banded hare wallaby
Petrogale xanthopus, Yellow-footed rock wallaby
Caloprymnus campestris, Desert rat kangaroo
Bettongia penicillata, Brush-tailed rat kangaroo
Bettongia lesueur, Lesueur's rat kangaroo
Bettongia tropica, Northern rat kangaroo
Bettongia gaimardi, Gaimard's rat kangaroo
Wyulda squamicaudata, Scaly-tailed possum
Gymnobelideus leadbeateri, Leadbeater's possum
Burramys parvus, Mountain pygmy possum
Dendrolagus inustus, Grizzled gray tree kangaroo
Dendrolagus ursinus, Black tree kangaroo
Lasiorhinus latifrons latifrons, Hairy-nosed wombat
Lasiorhinus barnardi, Barnard's hairy-nosed wombat
Lasiorhinus gillespiei, Queensland hairy-nosed wombat
Perameles bougainville, Barred bandicoot
Perameles eremiana, Desert bandicoot
Chaeropus ecaudatus, Pig-footed bandicoot
Macrotis lagotis, Rabbit bandicoot
Macrotis leucura, Lesser rabbit bandicoot
Dasyurus viverrinus, Eastern native cat
Phascogale calura, Red-tailed phascogale
Antechinus apicalis, Dibbler
Planigale tenuirostris, Southern planigale
Planigale subtilissima, Little planigale
Sminthopsis longicaudata, Long-tailed marsupial mouse
Sminthopsis psammophila, Large desert marsupial mouse
Antechinomys laniger, Eastern jerboa marsupial
Myrmecobius fasciatus rufus, Rusty numbat
Thylacinus cynocephalus, Thylacine

Insectivora
Atopogale cubana, Cuban solenodon
Solenodon paradoxus, Haitian solenodon
Erinaceus frontalis, Southern African hedgehog
Podogymnura truei, Mindanao gymnure
Desmana moschata, Russian desman
Galemys pyrenaicus, Pyrenean desman

Chiroptera
Myotis sodalis, Indiana bat
Lasiurus cinereus semotus, Hawaiian hoary bat
Corynorhinus townsendii ingens, Ozark big-eared bat
Corynorhinus townsendii virginianus, Virginian big-eared bat
Euderma maculatum, Spotted bat

Primates
Lemur, all species, True lemur
Lepilemur, all species, Weasel or sportive lemur
Hapalemur, all species, Gentle lemur
Allocebus, all species, Petter's mouse lemur
Cheirogaleus, all species, Dwarf lemur
Microcebus, all species, Mouse lemur
Phaner, all species, Fork-marked lemur
Indri, all species, Indris
Propithecus, all species, Sifaka
Avahi, all species, Woolly lemur
Daubentonia madagascariensis, Aye-aye
Nycticebus coucang, Slow loris
Loris tardigradus, Slender loris
Leontideus, all species, Golden lion marmoset
Callimico goeldii, Goeldi's marmoset
Chiropotes albinasus, White-nosed saki
Cacajao, all species, Uakari
Saimiri oerstedii, Costa Rican squirrel monkey
Cebus capucinus, White-throated capuchin
Alouatta palliata (villosa), Central American howler
Ateles geoffroyi frontatus, Costa Rican spider monkey
Ateles geoffroyi panamensis, Panamanian spider monkey
Brachyteles arachnoides, Woolly spider monkey
Cercocebus galeritus galeritus, Tana River mangabey
Macaca silenus, Lion-tailed macaque or Wanderoo
Macaca sylvanus, Barbary ape
Colobus badius rufomitratus, Red colobus
Colobus badius kirkii, Zanzibar red colobus
Colobus badius gordonorum, Uhehe red colobus
Colobus verus, Olive colobus
Presbytis johnii, John's langur
Presbytis geei, Golden langur
Presbytis pileatus, Capped langur
Presbytis entellus, Entellus langur
Simias concolor, Pagi Island or pig-tailed langur
Rhinopithecus roxellanae, Snub-nosed langur
Pygathrix nemaeus, Douc langur
Nasalis larvatus, Proboscis monkey
Hylobates, all species, Gibbon
Symphalangus syndactylus, Siamang
Pongo pygmaeus, Orangutan
Pan troglodytes, Chimpanzee
Pan paniscus, Pygmy chimpanzee
Gorilla gorilla, Gorilla

Edentata
Myrmecophaga tridactyla, Giant anteater
Bradypus torquatus, Brazilian three-toed sloth
Bradypus boliviensis, Bolivian three-toed sloth
Priodontes giganteus, Giant armadillo
Tolypeutes tricinctus, Brazilian three-banded armadillo
Chlamyphorus truncatus, Pink fairy armadillo
Burmeisteria retusa, Greater pichiciego
Tamandua tetradactyla chapadensis, Argentine tamandua

Pholidota
Manis temmincki, Cape pangolin
Manis crassicaudata, Indian pangolin
Manis pentadactyla, Chinese pangolin
Manis javanica, Malayan pangolin

Lagomorpha
Pentalagus furnessi, Ryukyu rabbit
Romerolagus diazi, Volcano rabbit
Caprolagus hispidus, Assam rabbit
Nesolagus netscheri, Sumatra short-eared rabbit

Rodentia
Sciurus niger cinereus, Dalmarva Peninsula fox
squirrel
Ratufa, all species, Giant squirrel
Epixerus ebii, Ebian's palm squirrel
Epixerus wilsoni, Wilson's palm squirrel
Lariscus hosei, Four-striped ground squirrel
Marmota menzbieri, Menzbier's marmot
Cynomys mexicanus, Mexican prairie dog
Cynomys parvidens, Utah prairie dog
Dipodomys elephantinus, Big-eared kangaroo rat
Dipodomys heermanni morroensis, Morro Bay
kangaroo rat
Dipodomys elator, Texas kangaroo rat
Dipodomys phillipsii phillipsii, Phillip's kangaroo rat
Castor fiber birulaia, Mongolian beaver
Castor canadensis mexicanus, Mexican beaver
Castor canadensis frondator, Broad-tailed beaver
Castor canadensis repentinus, Grand Canyon beaver
Zyzomys pedunculatus, Central thick-tailed rat
Leporillus conditor, Stick-nest or house-building rat
Pseudomys novaehollandiae, New Holland mouse
Pseudomys praeconis, Shark Bay mouse
Pseudomys shortridgei, Shortridge's mouse
Pseudomys fumeus, Smokey mouse
Pseudomys occidentalis, Western mouse
Pseudomys fieldi, Field's mouse
Pseudomys gouldii, Gould's mouse
Notomys aquilo, Gulf hopping mouse
Xeromys myoides, False water rat
Reithrodontomys raviventris, Salt-marsh harvest
mouse
Microtus pennsylvanicus provectus, Block Island
meadow vole
Microtus breweri, Beach meadow vole
Ondatra zibethicus bernardi, Colorado River muskrat
Tokudaia osimensis muenninki, Ryukyu spiny rat
Chaetomys subspinosus, Thin-spined porcupine
Chinchilla laniger, Chinchilla
Chinchilla brevicaudata boliviana, Bolivian chinchilla
Capromys melanurus, Bushy-tailed hutia
Capromys nana, Dwarf hutia
Geocapromys brownii, Jamaican hutia
Geocapromys ingrahami, Bahaman hutia
Plagiodontia aedium, Cuvier's hutia
Plagiodontia hylaeum, Dominican hutia

Cetacea
Platanista gangetica, Ganges freshwater
dolphin
Physeter catodon, Sperm whale
Eschrichtius robustus, Gray whale
Balaenoptera physalus, Finback whale
Balaenoptera musculus, Blue whale
Balaenoptera borealis, Sei whale
Megaptera novaeangliae, Humpback whale

Balaena mysticetus, Bowhead whale
Eubalaena, all species, Right whale

Carnivora
Canis lupus irremotus, Northern Rocky Mountain wolf
Canis lupus lycaon, Eastern timber wolf
Canis lupus monstrabilis, Mexican wolf
Canis lupus pallipes, Indian wolf
Canis lupus crassodon, Vancouver Island wolf
Canis rufus, Red wolf
Chrysocyon brachyurus, Maned wolf
Canis simensis simensis, Northern Simien fox
Vulpes velox hebes, Northern kit fox
Vulpes macrotis mutica, San Joaquín kit fox
Atelocynus microtis, Small-eared dog
Speothos venaticus, Bush dog
Cuon alpinus, Asiatic wild dog or dhole
Lycaon pictus, African wild dog
Tremarctos ornatus, Spectacled bear
Selenarctos thibetanus gedrosianus, Baluchistan bear
Ursus americanus emmonsii, Glacier bear
Ursus arctos, all North American and Italian
subspecies, Brown bear
Ursus arctos horribilis, Grizzly bear in lower 48 states
of U.S.
Ursus arctos nelsoni, Mexican grizzly bear
Ursus arctos richardsoni, Barren-ground grizzly bear
Ursus arctos pruinosus, Mongolian brown bear
Ursus maritimus, Polar bear
Helarctos malayanus, Malayan sun bear
Ailuropoda melanoleuca, Giant panda
Ailurus fulgens, Red panda
Martes americana atrata, Newfoundland pine marten
Martes flavigula chrysospila, Formosan yellow-
throated marten
Mustela nigripes, Black-footed ferret
Lutra felina, Marine otter
Lutra longicaudis, South American river otter
Lutra provocax, Southern river otter
Pteronura brasiliensis, Giant otter
Paraonyx microdon, Cameroon clawless otter
Enhydra lutris nereis, Southern sea otter
Viverra megaspila civettina, Malabar large-spotted
civet
Fossa fossa, Malagasy civet
Cynogale bennetti, Otter civet
Prionodon linsang, Banded linsang
Prionodon pardicolor, Spotted linsang
Helogale derbianus, Dwarf mongoose
Eupleres goudoti, Falanouc
Cryptoprocta ferox, Fossa
Hyaena brunnea, Brown hyena
Hyaena hyaena barbara, Barbary hyena
Felis lynx isabellina, Lynx
Felis lynx pardina, Spanish lynx
Felis caracal, Caracal lynx
Felis pardalis, Ocelot
Felis tigrina, Tiger cat
Felis colocolo, Three subspecies, Pampus cat
Felis nigripes, Black-footed cat
Felis yagouaroundi, Jaguarundi
Felis concolor cougar, Eastern cougar
Felis concolor coryi, Florida cougar
Felis concolor missoulensis, Canadian Rocky
Mountain cougar
Felis concolor myensis, Mexican cougar
Felis concolor azteca, Mexican cougar
Felis concolor costaricensis, Costa Rican cougar

Felis planiceps, Flat-headed cat
Felis temmincki, Temminck's golden cat
Felis bengalensis bengalensis, Indian leopard cat
Felis serval, Serval
Felis wiedii, Margay
Felis marmorata, Marbled cat
Felis jacobita, Andean cat
Felis (lynx) rufa escuinapae, Mexican bobcat
Neofelis nebulosa, Clouded leopard
Panthera tigris, Tiger
Panthera leo persica, Asiatic lion
Panthera pardus, Leopard
Panthera uncia, Snow leopard
Panthera onca, Jaguar
Acinonyx jubatus, Cheetah

Pinnipedia
Arctocephalus galapagoensis, Galápagos fur seal
Arctocephalus philippii, Juan Fernandez fur seal
Arctocephalus townsendi, Guadalupe fur seal
Arctocephalus australis, South American fur seal
Zalophus californianus japonicus, Japanese sea lion
Odobenus rosmarus laptevi, Laptev walrus
Phoca kurilensis, Kurile harbor seal
Phoca hispida saimensis, Saimaa seal
Monachus, all species, Monk seal
Mirounga angustirostris, Northern or Mexican
    elephant seal
Mirounga australis, South Atlantic elephant seal
Mirounga leonina, South Pacific elephant seal

Tubulidentata
Orycteropus afer, Aardvark

Proboscidea
Elephas maximus, Asian elephant

Sirenia
Dugong dugon, Dugong
Trichechus manatus, West Indian manatee
Trichechus inunguis, Amazon manatee
Trichechus senegalensis, West African manatee

Perissodactyla
Equus przewalskii, Przewalski's horse or Mongolian
    wild horse
Equus hemionus, Asiatic wild ass
Equus asinus, African wild ass
Equus zebra zebra, Cape mountain zebra
Tapirus pinchaque, Mountain tapir
Tapirus bairdii, Central American tapir
Tapirus indicus, Malayan tapir
Tapirus terrestris, South American tapir
Rhinoceros unicornis, Great Indian or great one-
    horned rhinoceros
Rhinoceros sondaicus, Javan rhinoceros
Didermoceros sumatrensis, Sumatran rhinoceros
Ceratotherium simum cottoni, Northern white
    rhinoceros
Diceros bicornis, Black rhinoceros

Artiodactyla
Sus salvanius, Pygmy hog
Babyrousa babyrussa, Babirusa
Choeropsis liberiensis, Pygmy hippopotamus
Vicugna vicugna, Vicuña
Camelus bactrianus, Wild Bactrian camel
Muntiacus crinifrons, Black muntjac

Muntiacus feae, Fea's muntjac
Dama mesopotamica, Persian fallow deer
Moschus moschiferus moschiferus, Indian musk deer
Axis (Hyelaphus) kuhlii, Kuhl's deer or Bawean Island
    deer
Axis (Hyelaphus) porcinus annamiticus, Thailand hog
    deer
Axis (Hyelaphus) calamianensis, Calamian Island deer
Cervus duvauceli, Swamp deer
Cervus eldi, Brow-antlered deer
Cervus eldi siamensis, Thailand brown-antlered deer
Cervus nippon taiouanus, Formosan sika
Cervus nippon keramae, Ryukyu sika
Cervus nippon mandarinensis, North China sika
Cervus nippon grassianus, Shansi sika
Cervus nippon kopschi, South China sika
Cervus albirostris, Thorold's deer
Cervus elaphus corsicanus, Corsican red deer
Cervus elaphus wallichi, Shou
Cervus elaphus barbarus, Barbary deer
Cervus elaphus hanglu, Kashmir stag or Hangul
Cervus elaphus yarkandensis, Yarkand deer
Cervus elaphus bactrianus, Bactrian deer
Cervus elaphus macneilli, MacNeill's deer
Cervus elaphus nannodes, Tule elk
Odocoileus virginianus clavium, Key deer
Odocoileus virginianus leucurus, Columbian white-
    tailed deer
Odocoileus hemionus cerrosensis, Cedros Island mule
    deer
Hippocamelus bisculcus, Chilean guemal
Hippocamelus antisensis, Peruvian guemal
Blastoceros dichotomus, Marsh deer or South
    American swamp deer
Ozotoceros bezoarticus, Pampas deer
Pudu mephistophiles, Pudu deer
Pudu pudu, Southern pudu deer
Antilocapra americana peninsularis, Lower or Baja
    California pronghorned antelope
Antilocapra americana sonoriensis, Sonoran
    pronghorned antelope
Antilocapra americana mexicana, Mexican
    pronghorned antelope
Taurotragus derbianus derbianus, Western giant eland
Bubalus bubalis, Asiatic buffalo
Anoa mindorensis, Tamarau
Anoa depressicornis, Lowland anoa
Anoa quarlesi, Mountain anoa
Bibos banteng, Banteng
Bos gaurus, Gaur
Bos sauveli, Kouprey
Bos (grunniens) mutus, Wild yak
Bison bonasus, European bison
Bison bison athabascae, Woodland bison
Cephalophus jentinki, Jentink's duiker
Cephalophus monticola, Blue duiker
Kobus leche smithemani, Black lechwe
Hippotragus niger variani, Giant sable antelope
Oryx leucoryx, Arabian oryx
Oryx dammah, Scimitar-horned oryx
Addax nasomaculatus, Addax
Damaliscus dorcas dorcas, Bontebok
Alcelaphus buselaphus tora, Tora hartebeest
Alcelaphus buselaphus swaynei, Swayne's hartebeest
Connochaetes gnou, Black wildebeest
Nesotragus moschatus moschatus, Zanzibar suni
Dorcatragus megalotis, Beira antelope
Saiga tatarica mongolica, Mongolian saiga antelope

Pantholops hodgsoni, Tibetan antelope
Aepyceros melampus petersi, Black-faced impala
Gazella subgutturosa marica, Sand gazelle
Gazella dorcas massaesyla, Moroccan dorcas gazelle
Gazella gazella, Mountain gazelle
Gazella cuvieri, Cuvier's gazelle
Gazella leptoceros, Slender-horned gazelle
Gazella dama mhorr, Mhorr gazelle
Gazella dama lozanoi, Rio de Oro dama gazelle
Nemorhaedus goral, Goral
Capricornis sumatraensis sumatraensis, Sumatran serow
Budorcas taxicolor tibetana, Szechwan takin
Budorcas taxicolor bedfordi, Golden takin
Hemitragus hylocrius, Nilgiri tahr
Hemitragus jayakari, Arabian tahr
Rupicapra rupicapra ornata, Italian chamois
Capra ibex walie, Walia ibex
Capra pyrenaica pyrenaica, Pyrenean ibex
Capra falconeri, Markhor
Capra falconeri jerdoni, Straight-horned markhor
Capra falconeri megaceros, Kabal markhor
Capra falconeri chiltanensis, Chiltan markhor
Ovis canadensis, Bighorn sheep
Ovis orientalis ophion, Cyprian urial sheep
Ovis ammon, Argali or Marco Polo sheep
Ovis vignei, Shapo sheep

AMPHIBIANS

Caudata
Andrias japonicus japonicus, Japanese giant salamander
Andrias japonicus davidianus, Chinese giant salamander
Ambystoma dumerili dumerili, Lake Patzcuaro salamander
Ambystoma lermaensis, Lake Lerma salamander
Ambystoma macrodactylum croceum, Santa Cruz long-toed salamander
Ambystoma mexicanum, Mexican axolotl
Chioglossa lusitanica, Gold-striped salamander
Batrachoseps aridus, Desert slender salamander
Batrachoseps simatus, Kern Canyon slender salamander
Batrachoseps stebbinsi, Tehachapi slender salamander
Phaeognathus hubrichti, Red hills salamander
Plethodon larselli, Larch mountain salamander
Plethodon nettingi, Cheat mountain salamander
Typhlotriton spelaeus, Grotto salamander
Typhlomolge rathbuni, Texas blind salamander
Haideotriton wallacei, Georgia blind salamander
Hydromantes shastae, Shasta salamander
Hydromantes brunus, Limestone salamander

REPTILES

Salientia
Leiopelma archeyi, Coromandel frog
Leiopelma hamiltoni, Stephen's Island frog
Leiopelma hochstetteri, North Island frog
Xenopus gilli, Cape clawed frog
Discoglossus nigriventer, Israel painted frog
Batrachophrynus macrostomus, Lake Junin frog
Bufo boreas nelsoni, Amargosa toad
Bufo boreas exsul, Black toad
Bufo houstonensis, Houston toad
Bufo retiformis, Sonoran green toad

Bufo superciliaris, Cameroon toad
Bufo periglenes, Monteverde toad
Nectophrynoides occidentalis, Mount Nimba viviparous toad
Nectophrynoides, other species, African viviparous toads
Atelopus varius zeteki, Panamanian golden frog
Hyla andersoni, Pine Barrens tree frog
Pseudacris streckeri illinoensis, Illinois chorus frog
Nesomantis thomasseti, Thomasset's Seychelles frog
Sooglossus seychellensis, Seychelles frog
Sooglossus gardineri, Gardiner's Seychelles frog
Rana pipiens fisheri, Vegas Valley leopard frog
Megalixalus seychellensis, Seychelles tree frog

Testudines
Batagur baska, Asian river terrapin
Chrysemys ornata callirostris, South American slider
Clemmys muhlenbergi, Bog turtle
Geoclemmys hamiltoni, Black pond turtle
Geomyda tricarinata, Three-keeled land turtle
Kachuga tecta tecta, Pakistan roofed turtle
Morenia ocellata, Burmese eyed turtle
Terrapene coahuila, Aquatic box turtle
Acinixys planicauda, Madagascar flat-shelled tortoise
Chersine angulata, Bowsprint tortoise
Geochelone elephantopus, Galápagos tortoise
Geochelone, other species, tortoises
Gopherus, agassizi, Desert tortoise
Gopherus berlandieri, Texas tortoise
Gopherus flavomarginatus, Mexican giant gopher tortoise
Gopherus polyphemus, Florida gopher tortoise
Homopus, all species, African tortoises
Kinixys, all species, hinged tortoises
Malacochersus tornieri, Pancake tortoise
Psammobates geometricus, Geometric tortoise
Pyxis arachnoides, Madagascar spider turtle
Testudo, all species, tortoises
Caretta caretta, Loggerhead turtle
Chelonia depressa, Flatback sea turtle
Chelonia mydas, Green turtle
Eretmochelys imbricata, Hawksbill turtle
Lepidochelys kempi, Atlantic ridley turtle
Lepidochelys olivacea, Pacific ridley turtle
Dermochelys coriacea, Leatherback turtle
Trionyx ater, Mexican soft-shelled turtle
Trionyx nigricans, Dark soft-shelled turtle
Trionyx gangeticus, Ganges soft-shelled turtle
Trionyx hurum, Peacock soft-shelled turtle
Podocnemis erythrocephala, Red-headed Amazon turtle
Podocnemis dumeriliana, Duméril's greaved turtle
Podocnemis expansa, South American river turtle
Podocnemis lewyana, Magdalena river turtle
Podocnemis madagascariensis, Madagascar greaved turtle
Podocnemis unifilis, Yellow-spotted Amazon turtle
Podocnemis sextuberculata, Yellow-headed sidenecked turtle
Podocnemis vogli, Orinoco greaved turtle
Lissemys punctate punctata, Spotted flap-shelled turtle
Pseudemydura umbrina, Australian short-necked swamp turtle

Crocodylia
Alligator mississippiensis, American alligator

Alligator sinensis, Chinese alligator
Caiman crocodilus, Spectacled caiman
Caiman latirostris, Broad-snouted caiman
Melanosuchus niger, Black caiman
Paleosuchus palpebrosus, Dwarf caiman
Paleosuchus trigonatus, Smooth-fronted caiman
Crocodylus acutus, American crocodile
Crocodylus cataphractus, African slender-snouted
  crocodile
Crocodylus intermedius, Orinoco crocodile
Crocodylus johnsoni, Johnston's crocodile
Crocodylus moreleti, Morelet's crocodile
Crocodylus niloticus, Nile crocodile
Crocodylus novaeguineae, New Guinea crocodile
Crocodylus novaeguineae mindorensis, Philippine
  crocodile
Crocodylus palustris palustris, Mugger crocodile
Crocodylus palustris kimbula, Ceylon mugger
  crocodile
Crocodylus porosus, Salt-water crocodile
Crocodylus rhombifer, Cuban crocodile
Crocodylus siamensis, Siamese crocodile
Osteolaemus tetraspis, African dwarf crocodile
Tomistoma schlegeli, False gavial
Gavialis gangeticus, Gharial

Rhynchocephalia
Sphenodon punctatus, Tuatara

Squamata
Oedura reticulata, Reticulated velvet gecko
Phelsuma quentheri, Round Island day gecko
Phelsuma newtoni, Rodriguez day gecko
Uroplatus, all species, Madagascar leaf-tailed geckos
Amphibolurus maculatus griseus, Spotted dragon
  lizard
Gonyocephalus spinipes, Dragon lizard
Hydrosaurus pustulatus, Sail-fin lizard
Amblyrhynchus cristatus, Galápagos marine iguana
Brachylophus fasciatus, Fijian iguana
Conolophus pallidus, Barrington land iguana
Conolophus subcristatus, Galápagos land iguana
Crotaphytus wislizeni silus, Blunt-nosed leopard
  lizard or San Joaquín leopard lizard
Cyclura baeolopha, Andros Island ground iguana
Cyclura carinata carinata, Turks and Caicos ground
  iguana
Cyclura carinata bartschi, Mayaguana iguana
Cyclura cornuta cornuta, Rhinoceros iguana
Cyclura cornuta stejnegeri, Mona Island rhinoceros
  iguana
Cyclura cristata, White Cay ground iguana
Cyclura figginsi, Exuma Island ground iguana
Cyclura inornata, Allen Cay ground iguana
Cyclura macleayi macleayi, Cuban ground iguana
Cyclura macleayi caymanensis, Cayman Island iguana
Cyclura macleayi lewisi, Grand Cayman iguana
Cyclura nuchalis, Aklins ground iguana
Cyclura pinquis, Anegada ground iguana
Cyclura ricordi, Ricord's ground iguana
Cyclura rileyi, Watlings Island ground iguana
Phrynosoma coronatum blainvillei, San Diego horned
  lizard
Lacerta filfolensis filfolensis, Filfola lizard
Lacerta sicula coerulea, Faraglione lizard
Ameiva polops, St. Croix ground lizard
Cnemidophorus hyperythrus, Orange-throated
  whiptail

Leiolopisma telfairi, Round Island skink
Macroscincus coctaei, Cape Verde giant skink
Scelotes braueri, Seychelles skink
Scelotes veseyfitzgeraldi, Seychelles skink
Tiliqua adelaidensis, Miniature blue-tongued skink
Gerrhonotus panamintinus, Panamint alligator lizard
Anniella pulchra nigra, Black legless lizard
Shinisaurus crocodilurus, Chinese crocodile lizard
Heloderma horridum, Mexican beaded lizard
Heloderma suspectum, Gila monster
Varanus komodoensis, Komodo monitor
Varanus flavescens, Yellow monitor
Varanus bengalensis, Bengal monitor
Varanus griseus, Asian Desert monitor
Varanus, other species, Monitors

Serpentes
Acrantophis dumerili, Duméril's boa
Acrantophis madagascariensis, Madagascar boa
Bolyeria multicarinata, Round Island boa
Casarea dussumieri, Round Island boa
Charina bottae umbratica, Southern rubber boa
Epicrates angulifer, Cuban boa
Epicrates inornatus, Puerto Rican boa
Epicrates subflavus, Jamaican boa
Epicrates cenchris cenchris, Rainbow boa
Eunectes notaeus, Yellow anaconda
Constrictor constrictor, Boa constrictor
Python molurus molurus, Indian python
Python molurus bivittatus, Burmese python
Sanzinia madagascariensis, Madagascar tree boa
Elaphe triaspis, Neo-tropical rat snake
Langaha nasuta, Madagascar rear-fanged snake
Masticophis flagellum ruddocki, San Joaquín whip-
  snake
Masticophis lateralis euryxanthus, Alameda striped
  racer
Natrix sipedon insularum, Lake Erie water snake
Thamnophis couchi gigas, Giant garter snake
Thamnophis couchi hammondi, Two-striped garter
  snake
Thamnophis sirtalis tetrataenia, San Francisco garter
  snake
Cyclagras gigas, False water cobra
Clelia clelia, Mussurana
Elachistodon westermanni, Indian egg-eating snake

BIRDS

Sphenisciformes
Spheniscus mendiculus, Galápagos penguin
Spheniscus demersus, Black-footed penguin

Struthioniformes
Struthio camelus syriacus, Arabian ostrich
Struthio camelus spatzi, West African ostrich

Rheiformes
Pterocnemia pennata, Darwin's rhea
Rhea americana albescens, Grey rhea

Tinamiformes
Tinamus solitarius, Solitary tinamou
Crypturellus atrocapillus atrocapillus, Black-headed
  tinamou
Crypturellus casiquiare, Barred tinamou
Rhynochotus rufescens rufescens, Rufous tinamou
Rhynochotus rufescens pallescens, Argentine tinamou

Rhynochotus rufescens maculicollis, Spotted-necked tinamou

Podicipediformes
Podilymbus gigas, Atitlán grebe or Giant pied-billed grebe
Podiceps andinus, Andean eared grebe
Podiceps taczanowskii, Junin grebe
Tachybaptus rufolavatus, Alaotra grebe
Rollandia micropterum, Titicaca grebe

Procellariiformes
Diomedea albatrus, Short-tailed albatross
Diomedea irrorata, Galápagos waved albatross
Pterodroma aterrima, Réunion petrel
Pterodroma cahow, Cahow
Pterodroma leucoptera longirostris, Japanese petrel
Pterodroma macgillivrayi, Macgillivray's petrel
Pterodroma phaeopygia phaeopygia, Dark-rumped petrel
Pterodroma phaeopygia sandwichensis, Hawaiian dark-rumped petrel
Puffinus puffinus newellii, Newell's Manx shear-water

Pelecaniformes
Pelecanus crispus, Dalmatian pelican
Pelecanus occidentalis carolinensis, Eastern brown pelican
Nannopterum harrisi, Galápagos flightless cormorant
Phalacrocorax carunculatus carunculatus, King shag
Sula abbotti, Abbott's booby
Fregata andrewsi, Frigate bird

Ciconiiformes
Egretta eulophotes, Chinese egret
Ciconia ciconia boyciana, Japanese white stork
Ciconia nigra, Black stork
Nipponia nippon, Japanese crested ibis
Thaumatibis gigantea, Giant ibis
Geronticus eremita, Waldrapp
Geronticus calvus, Bald ibis
Platalea leucorodia, European spoonbill
Phoenicopterus ruber chilensis, Chilean flamingo
Phoenicoparrus andinus, Andean flamingo
Phoenicoparrus jamesi, James flamingo

Anseriformes
Cairina scutulata, White-winged wood duck
Dendrocygna arborea, Cuban tree duck
Anser Albifrons gambelli, Tule white-fronted goose
Branta canadensis leucopareia, Aleutian Canada goose
Branta sandvicensis, Hawaiian goose or Nene
Branta ruficollis, Red-breasted goose
Cereopsis novae-hollandiae, Cape Barren goose or Cereopsis
Coscoroba coscoroba, Coscoroba
Sarkidiornis melanotos, Knob-billed goose
Anas aucklandica, Brown teal
Anas bernieri, Madagascar teal
Anas diazi, Mexican duck
Anas laysanensis, Laysan duck or Laysan teal
Anas wyvilliana, Hawaiian duck or Koloa
Anas oustaleta, Marianas mallard
Rhodonessa caryophyllacea, Pink-headed duck
Cygnus bewickii jankowskii, Jankowski swan
Cygnus melancoryphus, Black-necked swan

Falconiformes
Vultur gryphus, Andean condor
Gymnogyps californianus, California condor
Gypaëtus barbatus meridionalis, African lammergeyer
Circus maillardi maillardi, Réunion harrier
Accipiter fasciatus natalis, Christmas Island goshawk
Accipiter francesii pusillus, Anjouan Island sparrow hawk
Accipter striatus fringilloides, Cuba sharp-skinned hawk
Buteo galapagoensis, Galápagos hawk
Buteo solitarius, Hawaiian hawk
Pithecophaga jefferyi, Monkey-eating eagle
Aquila heliaca adalberti, Spanish imperial eagle
Aquila chrysaetos, Golden eagle
Haliaeetus leucocephalus leucocephalus, Southern bald eagle
Haliaeetus heliaca adalberti, Spanish imperial eagle
Haliaeetus albicilla groenlandicus, Greenland white-tailed eagle
Harpia harpyja, Harpy eagle
Rostrhamus sociabilis plumbeus, Florida Everglade kite
Chondrohierax uncinatus mirus, Grenada hook-billed kite
Chondrohierax wilsonii, Cuba hook-billed kite
Falco newtoni aldabranus, Aldabra kestrel
Falco araea, Seychelles kestrel
Falco fasciinucha, Teita falcon
Falco kreyenborgi, Kleinschmidt's falcon
Falco punctatus, Mauritius kestrel
Falco sparverius guadalupensis, Guadalupe kestrel
Falco peregrinus anatum, American peregrine falcon
Falco peregrinus peregrinus, European peregrine falcon
Falco peregrinus tundrius, Arctic peregrine falcon
Falco peregrinus babylonicus, Middle Eastern peregrine falcon

Galliformes
Megapodius laperouse laperouse, Marianas megapode
Megapodius laperouse senex, Palau megapode
Megapodius freycinet nicoba-riensis, Nicobar Island megapode
Megapodius freycinet abbotti, Little Nicobar Island megapode
Macrocephalon maleo, Maleo
Crax blumenbachii, Red-billed curassow
Crax rubra griscomi, Cozumel curassow
Oreophasis derbianus, Horned guan
Aburria pipile pipile, Trinidad piping-guan
Pipile jacutinga, Black-fronted piping-guan
Tympanuchus cupido attwateri, Attwater's prairie chicken
Tympanuchus cupido pinnatus, Greater prairie chicken
Colinus virginianus ridgwayi, Masked bobwhite
Francolinus ochropectus, Tadjoura francolin
Francolinus swierstrai, Swierstra's francolin
Tragopan blythi blythi, Blyth's tragopan
Tragopan blythi molesworthi, Tibetan Blyth's tragopan
Tragopan caboti, Cabot's tragopan
Tragopan melanocephalus, Western tragopan
Lophophorus lhuysii, Chinese monal
Lophophorus sclateri, Sclater's monal
Lophophorus impejanus, Himalayan monal
Mitu mitu mitu, Mitu

Tetraogallus tibetanus, Tibetan snowcock
Tetraogallus caspius, Persian snowcock
Gallus sonneratii, Sonnerat's junglefowl
Cyrtonyx montezumae montezumae, Montezuma quail
Cyrtonyx montezumae merriami, Merriam's quail
Cyrtonyx montezumae mearnsi, Mearns's quail
Argusianus argus, Great argus pheasant
Ithaginus cruentus, Blood pheasant
Crossoptilon crossoptilon, White-eared pheasant
Crossoptilon mantchuricum, Brown-eared pheasant
Lophura edwardsi, Edwards's pheasant
Lophura imperialis, Imperial pheasant
Lophura swinhoii, Swinhoe's pheasant
Syrmaticus ellioti, Elliot's pheasant
Syrmaticus humiae burmanicus, Burmese bar-tailed
  pheasant
Syrmaticus humiae humiae, Hume's bar-tailed
  pheasant
Syrmaticus mikado, Mikado pheasant
Catreus wallichii, Cheer pheasant
Polyplectron emphanum, Palawan peacock pheasant
Polyplectron malacense schliermacheri, Bornean
  peacock pheasant
Polyplectron malacense malacense, Malaysian
  peacock pheasant
Polyplectron germaini, Germain peacock pheasant
Polyplectron bicalcaratum, Grey peacock pheasant

Gruiformes
Grus americana, Whooping crane
Grus canadensis nesiotes, Cuban sandhill crane
Grus canadensis pratensis, Florida sandhill crane
Grus canadensis pulla, Mississippi sandhill crane
Grus japonensis, Japanese crane
Grus leucogeranus, Siberian white crane
Grus monacha, Hooded crane
Grus nigricollis, Black-necked crane
Grus vipio, White-naped crane
Rallus pectoralis muelleri, Auckland Island rail
Rallus longirostris obsoletus, California clapper rail
Rallus longirostris yumanensis, Yuma clapper rail
Rallus longirostris levipes, Light-footed clapper rail
Tricholimnas sylvestris, Lord Howe wood rail
Cyanolimnas cerverai, Zapata rail
Aramidopsis plateni, Platen's Celebes rail
Gallirallus australis hectori, Eastern weka
Nesophylax ater, Henderson Island rail
Laterallus jamaicensis jamaicensis, Jamaican black
  rail
Edithornis silvestris, San Cristobal mountain rail
Gallinula chloropus sandvicensis, Hawaiian gallinule
Notornis mantelli, Takahé
Fulica cornuta, Horned coot
Fulica americana alai, Hawaiian coot
Rhynochetos jubatus, Kagu
Choriotis nigriceps, Great Indian bustard
Pedionomus torquatus, Plains wanderer
Eupodotis bengalensis, Bengal floricon
Balearica regulorum, South and East African crowned
  crane
Chlamydotis undulata, Houbara bustard
Otis tarda, Great bustard

Charadriiformes
Thinornis novae-seelandiae, New Zealand shore
  plover
Numenius borealis, Eskimo curlew
Numenius tenuirostris, Slender-billed curlew

Numenius minutus, Little whimbrel
Coenocorypha aucklandica, Pacific Island snipe
Himantopus himantopus knudseni, Hawaiian stilt
Larus audouinii, Audouin's gull
Larus relictus, Khar turuut tsakhlai
Larus brunneicephalus, Brown-headed gull
Sterna albifrons browni, California least tern
Tringa guttifer, Nordmann's greenshank
Synthliboramphus wumizusume, Japanese ancient
  murrelet

Columbiformes
Treron australis griveaudi, Moheli green pigeon
Drepanoptila holosericea, Cloven-feathered dove
Ducula goliath, Giant imperial pigeon
Ducula mindorensis, Mindoro imperial pigeon
Hemiphaga novaeseelandiae chathamensis, Chatham
  Island pigeon
Columba palumbus azorica, Azores wood pigeon
Columba inornata wetmorei, Puerto Rico plain pigeon
Columba trocaz trocaz, Madeira long-toed pigeon
Columba trocaz bollii, Tenerife long-toed pigeon
Columba jouyi, Ryukyu wood pigeon
Nesoenas mayeri, Mauritius pink pigeon
Streptopelia picturata rostrata, Seychelles turtle dove
Streptopelia reichenowi, White-winged dove
Leptotila wellsi, Grenada dove
Gallicolumba canifrons, Palau ground dove
Gallicolumba rubescens, Marquesas ground dove
Gallicolumba luzonica, Bleeding-heart pigeon
Goura victoria, Victoria crowned pigeon
Goura scheepmakeri, Sheepmaker's crowned pigeon
Goura cristata, Great crowned pigeon
Didunculus strigirostris, Tooth-billed pigeon
Caloenas nicobarica pelewensis, Palau nicobar pigeon

Psittaciformes
Strigops habroptilus, Kakapo or Owl parrot
Vini peruviana, Tahiti blue lory
Vini ultramarina, Ultramarine lory
Rhynchopsitta pachyrhyncha pachyrhyncha, Thick-
  billed parrot
Rhynchopsitta pachyrhyncha terrisi, Maroon-fronted
  parrot
Amazona guildingii, St. Vincent parrot
Amazona imperialis, Imperial parrot
Amazona leucocephala bahamensis, Bahamas parrot
Amazona versicolor, St. Lucia parrot
Amazona vittata, Puerto Rican parrot
Amazona rhodocorytha, Red-browed parrot
Amazona petrei petrei, Red-spectacled parrot
Amazona vinacea, Vinaceous breasted parrot
Anodorhynchus leari, Indigo macaw or Lear's macaw
Anodorhynchus glaucus, Glaucous macaw
Cyanopsitta spixii, Little blue macaw
Aratinga guaruba, Golden conure or Golden parakeet
Pyrrhura cruentata, Ochre-marked parakeet
Coracopsis nigra barklyi, Seychelles Vasa parrot
Psittacula krameri echo, Mauritius ring-necked
  parakeet
Prosopeia personata, Masked parakeet
Psephotus chrysopterygius chrysopterygius, Golden-
  shouldered parrot
Psephotus chrysopterygius dissimilis, Hooded parrot
Psephotus pulcherrimus, Paradise parrot
Neophema chrysogaster, Orange-bellied parrot
Neophema pulchella, Turquoise parrot
Neophema splendida, Scarlet-chested parrot

Eunymphicus cornutus cornutus, Horned parakeet
Eunymphicus cornutus uvaeensis, Loyalty Islands parakeet
Cyanoramphus auriceps forbesi, Forbe's parakeet
Cyanoramphus malherbi, Orange-fronted parakeet
Cyanoramphus novaezelandiae cookii, Norfolk Island parakeet
Cyanoramphus unicolor, Antipodes Island parakeet
Pezoporus wallicus flaviventris, Southwest Australian ground parrot
Pezoporus wallicus leachi, Tasmania ground parrot
Pezoporus wallicus wallicus, Southeast Australian ground parrot
Geopsittacus occidentalis, Night parrot
Pionopsitta pileata, Red-capped parrot
Psittacus erithacus princeps, Principe parrot
Poicephalus robustus, Brown-necked parrot
Tanygnathus luzoniensis, Blue-naped parrot
Probosciger alterrimus, Palm cockatoo

Cuculiformes
Tauraco ruspolii, Prince Ruspoli's touraco
Tauraco corythaix, White-crested touraco
Gallirex porphyreolophus, Purple-crested touraco
Coccyzus minor ferrugineus, Cocos mangrove cuckoo
Phaenicophaeus pyrrhocephalus, Red-faced malkoha

Strigiformes
Tyto soumagnei, Soumagne's owl
Otus gurneyi, Giant scops owl
Otus insularis, Seychelles owl
Otus nudipes newtoni, Virgin Islands screech owl
Otus podargina, Palau owl
Otus ireneae, Mrs. Morden's owlet
Sceloglaux albifacies albifacies, New Zealand laughing owl
Asio flammeus portoricensis, Puerto Rico short-eared owl
Otus rutilus capnodes, Anjouan scops owl

Caprimulgiformes
Siphonorhis americanus brewsteri, Hispaniola least pauraque
Caprimulgus noctitherus, Puerto Rico whippoorwill

Apodiformes
Apus myoptilus, Scarce swift
Apus toulsoni, Luanda swift
Micropanyptila furcata furcata, Pygmy swift
Ramphodon dohrnii, Hook-billed hermit

(N.B. The hummingbirds listed below appear to have a very restricted distribution in the countries mentioned, and seem to be rare, although their precise status remains unknown.)
Phaethornis porcullae, Peru
Goldmania violiceps, Panama
Goethalsia bella, Panama
Amazilia castaneiventris, Colombia
Amazilia cyaneotincta, Colombia
Amazilia hollandi, Venezuela
Amazilia luciae, Honduras
Phlogophilus harterti, Peru
Hylonympha macrocerca, Venezuela
Metallura malagae, Bolivia

Augastes lumachellus, Brazil
Loddigesia mirabilis, Peru

Trogoniformes
Pharomachrus mocinno, Resplendent quetzal

Coraciiformes
Uratelornis chimaera, Long-tailed ground roller
Buceros bicornis, Great Indian hornbill
Buceros rhinoceros rhinoceros, Malayan rhinoceros hornbill
Buceros hydrocorax hydrocorax, Rufous hornbill
Rhinoplax vigil, Helmeted hornbill
Aceros narcondami, Narcondam hornbill

Piciformes
Dryocopus javensis richardsi, Tristram's woodpecker
Melanerpes superciliaris bahamensis, Grand Bahama red-bellied woodpecker
Melanerpes superciliaris blakei, Abaco red-bellied woodpecker
Melanerpes superciliaris nyeanus, Watlings Island red-bellied woodpecker
Sapheopipo noguchii, Okinawa woodpecker
Dendrocopus borealis, Red-cockaded woodpecker
Campephilus principalis bairdii, Cuban ivory-billed woodpecker
Campephilus principalis principalis, Ivory-billed woodpecker
Campephilus imperialis, Imperial woodpecker
Picus squamatus flavirostris, Transcaspian scaly-bellied green woodpecker

Passeriformes
Aphrastura masafuerae, Masafuera creeper
Asthenes sclateri, Sclater's spinetail
Myrmotherula erythronotos, Red-rumped ant-thrush
Rupicola rupicola, Guianan Cock-of-the-Rock
Rupicola peruviana, Andean Cock-of-the-Rock
Empidonax euleri johnstonei, Euler's flycatcher
Nesotriccus ridgwayi, Cocos Island flycatcher
Pitta kochi, Koch's pitta
Pitta brachyura nympha, Formosan blue-winged pitta
Xenicus longipes longipes, South Island bush wren
Xenicus longipes stokesi, North Island bush wren
Xenicus longipes variabilis, Stead's bush wren or Stewart Island bush wren
Neodrepanis hypoxantha, Small-billed false sunbird
Atrichornis clamosus, Noisy scrub-bird
Atrichornis rufescens, Rufous scrub-bird
Alauda razae, Raza Island lark
Malaconotus kupeensis, Kupé mountain bush shrike
Aplonis fuscus fuscus, Norfolk Island starling
Aplonis pelzelni, Ponapé mountain starling
Leucopsar rothschildi, Rothschild's starling or myna
Callaeas cinerea, Kokako
Creadion carunculatus, Saddleback
Turnagra capensis, Piopio
Corvus tropicus, Hawaiian crow
Coracina graueri, Grauer's cuckoo shrike
Coquus newtoni, Réunion cuckoo shrike
Coquus typicus, Mauritius cuckoo shrike
Salpinctes obsoletus guadeloupensis, Guadaloupe rock wren
Thryomanes sissonii, Socorro Island wren
Troglodytes aëdon mesoleucus, St. Lucia wren
Troglodytes aëdon guadeloupensis, Guadaloupe house wren

Troglodytes aëdon musicus, St. Vincent wren
Troglodytes troglodytes alascensis, Pribilov wren
Troglodytes troglodytes fridariensis, Fair Isle wren
Troglodytes troglodytes hirtensis, St. Kilda wren
Nesomimus trifasciatus trifasciatus, Charles Island mockingbird
Mimodes graysoni, Socorro Island thrasher
Cinclocerthia ruficauda gutturalis, Martinique brown trembler
Ramphocinclus brachyurus brachyurus, Martinique white-breasted thrasher
Ramphocinclus brachyurus sanctae-luciae, St. Lucia white-breasted thrasher
Phyllastrephus orostruthus amani, Tanzania dappled bulbul
Phyllastrephus orostruthus orostruthus, Dappled bulbul
Hypsipetes borbonicus olivaceus, Mauritius olivaceous bulbul
Erithacus ruficeps, Rufous-headed robin
Copsychus niger cebuensis, Cebu black shama thrush
Copsychus seychellarum, Seychelles magpie-robin
Myadestes elisabeth retrusus, Isle of Pines solitaire
Myadestes genibarbis sibilans, St. Vincent thrush
Zoothera cinerea, Ashy ground thrush
Nesocichla eremita eremita, Tristan starchy
Nesocichla eremita gordoni, Inaccesible Island starchy
Nesocichla eremita procax, Nightingale Island starchy
Phaeornis obscurus myadestina, Large Kauai thrush
Phaeornis obscurus rutha, Molokai thrush
Phaeornis palmeri, Puaiohi
Turdus helleri, Teita olive thrush
Turdus poliocephalus poliocephalus, Gray-headed blackbird
Turdus ravidus, Grand Cayman thrush
Cichlherminia l'herminieri sanctae-luciae, St. Lucia forest thrush
Psophodes nigrogularis, Western whipbird
Paradoxornis heudei, Lower Yangtze Kiang crow tit
Picathartes gymnocephalus, White-necked rock-fowl
Picathartes oreas, Gray-necked rock-fowl
Bebrornis rodericanus, Rodriguez warbler
Bebrornis sechellensis, Seychelles warbler
Acrocephalus kingi, Nihoa miller-bird
Acrocephalus luscinia rehsei, Nauru nightingale warbler
Sericornis nigroviridis, Watut leaf warbler
Dasyornis brachypterus longirostris, Western bristlebird
Dasyornis broadbenti littoralis, Western rufous bristlebird
Bowdleria punctata wilsoni, Codfish Island fernbird
Amytornis goyderi, Eyrean grass-wren
Regulus calendula obscura, Guadeloupe kinglet
Muscicapa ruecki, Rueck's blue flycatcher
Rhipidura lepida, Palau fantail
Petroica traversi, Chatham Island robin
Petroica multicolor multicolor, Scarlet-breasted robin
Pomarea nigra nigra, Tahiti flycatcher
Pomarea nigra pomarea, Maupiti Island flycatcher
Terpsiphone bourbonnensis, Coq de bois
Terpsiphone corvina, Seychelles black flycatcher
Metabolus rugensis, Truk monarch
Monarcha takatsukasae, Tinian monarch flycatcher
Moho braccatus, Kauai oo honeyeater
Notiomystis cincta, Stitchbird

Prosthemadera novaeseelandiae chathamensis, Chatham Island tui
Meliphaga cassidix, Helmeted honeyeater
Rukia ruki, Truk great white-eye
Rukia sanfordi, Ponapé great white-eye
Speirops brunnea, Fernando Po speirops
Zosterops modestus, Seychelles white-eye
Zosterops albogularis, White-breasted silver-eye
Vireo gracilirostris, Slender-billed vireo
Loxops maculata flammea, Molokai creeper
Loxops maculata bairdi, Kauai alauwahio
Loxops coccinea ochraceu, Maui akepa
Loxops maculata maculata, Oahu creeper
Loxops maculata mana, Hawaii creeper
Loxops maculata newtoni, Maui creeper
Loxops coccinea coccinea, Hawaii akepa
Hemignathus lucidus hanapepe, Kauai nukupuu honeycreeper
Hemignathus lucidus affinus, Maui nukupuu honeycreeper
Hemignathus procerus, Kauai akialoa
Hemignathus wilsoni, Hawaiian nukupuu
Pseudonestor xanthophrys, Maui parrotbill
Psittirostra bailleui, Palila honeycreeper
Psittirostra cantans cantans, Laysan finch
Psittirostra psittacea, Ou honeycreeper
Palmeria dolei, Crested honeycreeper
Leucopeza semperi, Semper's warbler
Vermivora bachmanii, Bachman's warbler
Dendroica kirtlandii, Kirtland's warbler
Dendroica petechia aureola, Cocos yellow warbler
Dendroica petechia petechia, Barbados yellow warbler
Foudia sechellarum, Seychelles fody
Foudia rubra, Mauritius fody
Erythrura kleinschmidti, Pink-billed parrot finch
Carpodacus amplus, Guadeloupe house finch
Carpodacus mcgregori, McGregor's house finch
Pinaroloxias inornata, Cocos Island finch
Paroaria baeri, Baer's cardinal
Sporophila insulata, Tumaco seedeater
Pyrrhula pyrrhula murina, São Miguel bullfinch
Warsanglia johannis, Warsangli linnet
Nesospiza acunhae acunhae, Tristan bunting
Nesospiza acunhae questi, Nightingale Island bunting
Nesospiza wilkinsi dunnei, Inaccesible Island bunting
Nesospiza wilkinsi wilkinsi, Wilkins' bunting
Geospiza magnirostris magnirostris, Charles Island ground finch
Tangavius armenti, Colombian red-eyed cowbird
Cassidix nicaraguensis, Nicaragua grackle
Cassidix palustris, Slender-billed grackle
Icterus leucopteryx bairdi, Grand Cayman troupial
Pipilo socorroensis, Socorro towhee
Passerculus princeps, Ipswich sparrow
Torreornis inexpectata inexpectata, Zapata sparrow
Torreornis inexpectata sigmani, Oriente sparrow
Ammospiza mirabilis, Cape Sable sparrow
Ammospiza nigrescens, Dusky seaside sparrow
Junco insularis, Guadeloupe junco
Compsospiza baeri, Baer's mountain finch
Compsospiza garleppi, Garlepp's mountain finch
Pseudochelidon sirintarae, White-eyed river martin
Spinus yarellii, Yellow-faced siskin
Spinus cucullatus, Red siskin
Cotinga maculata, Banded cotinga
Xipholena atro-purpurea, White-winged cotinga
Melospiza melodia graminea, Santa Barbara sparrow
Melamprosps phaeosoma, Po'o uli

Acknowledgments

The editors of this volume are particularly indebted to the following staff members of the New York Zoological Park, Bronx, New York: William G. Conway, General Director; Joseph A. Davis, Scientific Assistant to the Director; and Wayne King, Curator of Herpetology. They also wish to thank: Earl Baysinger, Assistant Chief, Office of Endangered Species and International Activities of the Bureau of Sport Fisheries and Wildlife, U.S. Department of the Interior, Washington, D.C.; John Behler, Department of Herpetology, New York Zoological Park; Wayne Bohl, Office of Endangered Species and International Activities of the Bureau of Sport Fisheries and Wildlife, U.S. Department of the Interior; Arden H. Brame Jr., Supervisor, Eaton Canyon Nature Center, Pasadena, California, and Chairman of the Society for the Study of Amphibians and Reptiles; Donald F. Bruning, Curator of Ornithology, New York Zoological Park; Howard Campbell, Office of Endangered Species and International Activities of the Bureau of Sport Fisheries and Wildlife, U.S. Department of the Interior; Michael Carey, Busch Gardens, Tampa, Florida; Peter Crowcroft, Director, Chicago Zoological Park, Brookfield, Illinois; James Doherty, Curator of Mammalogy, New York Zoological Park; John F. Eisenberg, National Zoological Park, Washington, D.C.; Carl Gans, Department of Zoology, University of Michigan, Ann Arbor, Michigan; Nancy Genet, Garrison, New York; Edalee Harwell, Zoological Society of San Diego, San Diego, California; Marshall Howe, Office of Endangered Species and International Activities of the Bureau of Sport Fisheries and Wildlife, U.S. Department of the Interior; David Marshall, Office of Endangered Species and International Activities of the Bureau of Sport Fisheries and Wildlife, U.S. Department of the Interior; Robert H. Mattlin, Director, Overton Park Zoo, Memphis, Tennessee; Richard F. Myers, Raytown, Missouri; G. G. Montgomery, National Zoological Park, Washington, D.C.; Oklahoma City Zoo, Oklahoma City, Oklahoma; John Paradiso, Office of Endangered Species and International Activities of the Bureau of Sport Fisheries and Wildlife, U.S. Department of the Interior; Dorothy Revell, New York Zoological Park; Paul W. Sykes Jr., Endangered Wildlife Research Program, Bureau of Sport Fisheries and Wildlife, Delray Beach, Florida; Warren D. Thomas, Director, Gladys Porter Zoo, Brownsville, Texas; F. R. Walther, Department of Wildlife Science, College of Agriculture, Texas A&M University, College Station, Texas.

Picture Credits

Sources for the pictures in this book are shown below. Credits from left to right are separated by semicolons, from top to bottom by dashes.

13, 16, 21—Drawings by Thomas B. Allen.

Mammals

27—Jim Cooper, Victorian Fisheries and Wildlife Department. 28—John Dominis, TIME-LIFE Picture Agency, © 1972 Time Incorporated. 29—Robin Smith from The Photographic Library of Australia—Vincent Serventy from The Photographic Library of Australia. 30—Vincent Serventy from The Photographic Library of Australia. 31—Graham Pizzey from Bruce Coleman Ltd.—San Diego Zoo. 32—H. Millen, Sydney. 33—Frank W. Lane. 34—Vincent Serventy from Bruce Coleman Ltd. 35—Vincent Serventy from Bruce Coleman Inc. 37—Okapia, Frankfurt. 38—Richard F. Myers. 39—Nina Leen, TIME-LIFE Picture Agency, © 1972 Time Incorporated. 41—George Holton, © 1971. 42—Dr. Warren D. Thomas courtesy Gladys Porter Zoo. 43—Co Rentmeester, TIME-LIFE Picture Agency, © 1972 Time Incorporated. 44, 45—George Holton, © 1971. 46—Alan Anderson. 47—Carlo Bavagnoli, TIME-LIFE Picture Agency, © 1972 Time Incorporated. 48—Nina Leen, TIME-LIFE Picture Agency, © 1972 Time Incorporated. 49—Paul de Prins courtesy Cologne Zoo. 50, 51—Nina Leen, TIME-LIFE Picture Agency, © 1972 Time Incorporated. 52—San Diego Zoo. 53—Nina Leen, TIME-LIFE Picture Agency, © 1972 Time Incorporated. 54 through 62—Loomis Dean, TIME-LIFE Picture Agency, © 1972 Time Incorporated. 63—Carlo Bavagnoli, TIME-LIFE Picture Agency, © 1972 Time Incorporated. 65—Photograph by Jan Lindblad from his forthcoming book. 66—Claudia Andujar. 67—Dr. Estanislau Kostka Pinto da Silveira. 69 through 71—Nina Leen. 73—Dmitri Kessel, TIME-LIFE Picture Agency, © 1972 Time Incorporated. 74, 75—Juan Fernandez from Bruce Coleman Ltd. 76, 77—Nina Leen, TIME-LIFE Picture Agency, © 1972 Time Incorporated; Nina Leen. 78—Loomis Dean, TIME-LIFE Picture Agency, © 1972 Time Incorporated. 79—B. J. Rose. 80—C. Wemmer, Chicago Zoological Society. 81—San Diego Zoo. 82—Nina Leen, TIME-LIFE Picture Agency, © 1972 Time Incorporated—Bill Ray, TIME-LIFE Picture Agency, © 1972 Time Incorporated. 83—Oklahoma Zoo. 84—Patricia Caulfield. 86, 87—George B. Schaller courtesy New York Zoological Society; Dr. Stephen Berwick. 88—Leonard Lee Rue III. 89—Bruce Coleman Inc. 90, 91—John Dominis, TIME-LIFE Picture Agency, © 1972 Time Incorporated. 92, 93—Goetz D. Plage from Bruce Coleman Inc. 94—San Diego Zoo. 95—Stan Wayman, TIME-LIFE Picture Agency, © 1972 Time Incorporated. 96, 97—Photograph by Jan Lindblad from his forthcoming book. 98—Nina Leen—Frank W. Lane. 99—John Dominis, TIME-LIFE Picture Agency, © 1972 Time Incorporated. 101—Robert Evans. 102, 103—John Dominis, TIME-LIFE Picture Agency, © 1972 Time Incorporated. 104—George Laycock. 105—Ron Church from Photography Unlimited. 106, 107—Co Rentmeester, TIME-LIFE Picture Agency, © 1972 Time Incorporated. 108—Jen and Des Bartlett from Bruce Coleman Inc. 109—James A. Powell Jr. 110, 111—Dr. J. F. Eisenberg courtesy The National Zoological Park, Smithsonian Institution. 113—Wildlife Photographers (M.A.) from Bruce Coleman Inc. 114—Eliot Elisofon, TIME-LIFE Picture Agency, © 1972 Time Incorporated. 115—Christian Zuber from Rapho Guillumette; Nina Leen, TIME-LIFE Picture Agency, © 1972 Time Incorporated. 116—Frank W. Lane. 117—Carlo Bavagnoli, TIME-LIFE Picture Agency, © 1972 Time Incorporated. 118—Nina Leen, TIME-LIFE Picture Agency, © 1972 Time Incorporated. 119—Stephen O. Frankfurt. 121—F. R. Walther. 122, 123—Bill Ray, TIME-LIFE Picture Agency, © 1972 Time Incorporated. 124, 125—Dr. Richard Bell; Kenneth W. Fink from Bruce Coleman Inc. 126—Dr. Warren D. Thomas courtesy Gladys Porter Zoo—Nina Leen, TIME-LIFE Picture Agency, © 1972 Time Incorporated. 127—Peter Jackson from Bruce Coleman Ltd. 128—George B. Schaller from Bruce Coleman Inc.—W. T. Miller from Frank W. Lane. 129—Bob Peterson, TIME-LIFE Picture Agency, © 1972 Time Incorporated. 130—Oklahoma Zoo. 131—Robert H. Mattlin courtesy Overton Park Zoo—Patricia Caulfield, © 1973 Animals Animals. 132—F. R. Walther. 133—William L. Franklin. 134—Bruce Coleman Inc. 135—Nina Leen, TIME-LIFE Picture Agency, © 1972 Time Incorporated. 136—George B. Schaller from Bruce Coleman Inc. 137—Nina Leen. 138—Joe Van Wormer from Bruce Coleman Inc. 139—Patricia Caulfield. 140, 141—Carlo Bavagnoli, TIME-LIFE Picture Agency, © 1972 Time Incorporated.

Amphibians and Reptiles

145, 146—New York Zoological Society. 147—Nathan W. Cohen. 148, 149—Robert W. Mitchell. 150—Arden H. Brame Jr. 151, 152—Nathan W. Cohen. 153—New York Zoological Society. 155—Nina Leen, TIME-LIFE Picture Agency, © 1972 Time Incorporated. 156—David Hughes from Bruce Coleman Ltd.—Patricia Caulfield. 157—Frank W. Lane. 158—Nadine Z. from Rapho Guillumette. 159—David Hughes from Bruce Coleman Inc. 160, 161—Larry Burrows, TIME-LIFE Picture Agency, © 1972 Time Incorporated. 163—Vincent Serventy from Bruce Coleman Inc. 164, 165—Eliot Elisofon, TIME-LIFE Picture Agency, © 1972 Time Incorporated; John Wallis from Bruce Coleman Ltd. 166—Lynn Pelham from Rapho Guillumette, TIME-LIFE Picture Agency, © 1972 Time Incorporated. 167—Frank W. Lane. 168—John Markham from Bruce Coleman Inc. 169—Jane Burton from Bruce Coleman Ltd. 171—David Moore from Black Star for The Photographic Library of Australia. 173—Eric Hosking, F.R.P.S. 174—Nathan W. Cohen. 175—Merritt S. Keasey III. 176, 177—Larry Burrows, TIME-LIFE Picture Agency, © 1972 Time Incorporated. 178, 179—Nathan W. Cohen. 180—Norman Tomalin from Bruce Coleman Inc. 181—S. C. Bisserot from Bruce Coleman Inc. 183—W. D. Haacke. 184—Merritt S. Keasey III. 185—Nathan W. Cohen. 186—S. C. Bisserot from Bruce Coleman Inc. 187—Nathan W. Cohen.

Birds

191–Vernon Merritt III, TIME-LIFE Picture Agency, © 1972 Time Incorporated. 192–Eric Hosking, F.R.P.S. 193–George Laycock. 194, 195–George Holton. 196, 197 –David G. Allen, Bird Photographs Incorporated, Ithaca, N.Y. 198–Ron Johns from Bruce Coleman Inc. 199–Kojo Tanaka. 200–Maitland Edey. 201–New York Zoological Society. 202–Helen Cruickshank from National Audubon Society. 203–Ron Church from Photography Unlimited. 205–Kenneth W. Fink from Bruce Coleman Inc. 207–Eliot Elisofon, TIME-LIFE Picture Agency, © 1972 Time Incorporated. 208 –Eric Hosking, F.R.P.S.–New York Zoological Society. 209–Kenneth W. Fink from Ardea Photographics. 210–Thase Daniel. 211–B. J. Rose. 213–J. Scherschel, TIME-LIFE Picture Agency, © 1972 Time Incorporated. 214, 215–Kojo Tanaka, Animals Animals © 1972. 216 –Nina Leen, TIME-LIFE Picture Agency, © 1972 Time Incorporated. 217–Nina Leen. 218–New Zealand Wildlife Service–Arthur A. Allen, Bird Photographs Incorporated, Ithaca, N.Y., courtesy U.S. Bureau of Sport Fisheries and Wildlife. 219–Rajesh Bedi courtesy The Bikaner Zoo, Rajasthan, India. 221–Ray Erickson courtesy U.S. Fish and Wildlife Service. 222 –G. Harrison from Bruce Coleman Inc.–New York Zoological Society. 223–Sandy Sprunt from National Audubon Society. 224–San Diego Zoo. 225–John Markham from Bruce Coleman Inc. 226–Tony Beamish. 227–Larry Burrows, TIME-LIFE Picture Agency, © 1972 Time Incorporated. 229–New York Zoological Society. 230, 231–James A. Kern. 233–Eric Hosking, F.R.P.S. 234–E. McNamara from Ardea Photographics. 235–Nina Leen, TIME-LIFE Picture Agency, © 1972 Time Incorporated–Christopher Mylne, F.R.P.S., from Ardea Photographics. 236–George Laycock. 237–Photograph by Jan Lindblad from his forthcoming book. 239–Bill Ray, TIME-LIFE Picture Agency, © 1972 Time Incorporated. 240–David G. Allen, Bird Photographs Incorporated, Ithaca, N.Y. 241–Tony Beamish–Eric Hosking, F.R.P.S. 242, 243–John Dominis, TIME-LIFE Picture Agency, © 1972 Time Incorporated. 244, 245 –Frederick Kent Truslow from National Audubon Society; Patricia Caulfield. 246–Eric Hosking, F.R.P.S. –Ed N. Harrison, in the Library of the Western Foundation of Vertebrate Zoology. 247–Leonard McCombe, TIME-LIFE Picture Agency, © 1972 Time Incorporated.

INDEX

Numerals in italics indicate a
photograph or drawing of the subject
mentioned.

A

Addax (*Addax nasomaculatus*), *131*
Africa, 11, 19, 20, 40, 44, 54, 110, 112, 165, 204
Albatross, waved (*Diomedea irrorata*), 190, *194-195*
Alligator(s), 143, 162, 166, 168; American (*Alligator
   mississippiensis*), *166*; Chinese (*Alligator sinensis*),
   168
Amazon forest (Brazil), 11-12, 224, 236
Amazon River (South America), 40
Amphibians, 144-153
Andes, 98, 204
Angola, 141
Antarctica, 18, 84, 220, 232
Anteater, giant (*Myrmecophaga tridactyla*), 64, *65*
Antelope, 19, 20, 120; giant sable (*Hippotragus niger
   variani*), *140-141*
Ape(s), 40-45, 54
Arabian Peninsula, 20, 132
Aransas National Wildlife Refuge (Texas), 212
Arctic, 18
Argentina, 14, 204
Armadillo, three-banded (*Tolypeutes tricinctus*), 64, *66*
Asia, 26, 40, 42, 54, 90, 110, 111, 112, 116, 206, 212, 228
Ass(es): African (Ethiopian) wild (*Equus asinus*), 15,
   112, *117*; Asian wild (*Equus hemionus*), 112, *116*
Atlantic Ocean, 103, 168
Atlas Mountains (Africa), 132
Australia, 11, 14, 20, 26, 29, 30, 31, 34, 84, 156, 162, 190,
   220, 224, 225
Avahi, western woolly (*Avahi laniger occidentalis*), *54-
   55*
Aye-Aye (*Daubentonia madagascariensis*), 54, *63*

B

Bali-Barat Reserve (Indonesia), 232
Bandicoot, rabbit (*Macrotis lagotis*), 28
Bangweulu Plain (Africa), 124
Bat(s), 36, 38-39, 212; Indiana (*Myotis sodalis*), *38*;
   spotted (*Euderma maculatum*), *39*
Bear(s): polar (*Ursus maritimus*), 18, 100, *106-107*;
   spectacled (*Tremarctos ornatus*), 98
Beaver(s), 25, 68
Birds, 18, 143, 188-247
Bison: American, 15; long-horned, 25
Boa, Madagascar (*Acranthopis madagascariensis*),
   183
Bobwhite, masked (*Colinus virginianus ridgwayi*), 206,
   210
Bolivia, 204
Bontebok (*Damaliscus dorcas dorcas*), *128*
Borneo, 228
Brazil, 11-12, 46, 64, 67
Brisbane (Australia), 234
Burma, 168
Bustard, great Indian (*Choriotis nigriceps*), 212, *219*

C

Caiman(s), 162; spectacled (*Caiman crocodilus
   crocodilus*), 169; Yacaré (*Caiman crocodilus yacare*),
   167
Camel, 25, 120
Canada, 94, 129, 210, 212
Carnivores, 56; large, 84-99; small, 72-83
Cat(s): black-footed (*Felis nigripes*), *76*; eastern native
   (*Dasyurus viverrinus*), *31*; saber-toothed, 25
Ceylon. *See* Sri Lanka
Chad, 135
Cheetah(s) (*Acinonyx jubatus*), 14, 72, 84, *90-91*
Chile, 14
Chimpanzee(s) (*Pan troglodytes*), 40, *44-45*
China, 98, 206, 208, 214
Chinchilla, 68
Civet(s): Malagasy (*Fossa fossa*), 72, 80; otter
   (*Cynogale bennetti*), *81*
Cock-of-the-rock (*Rupicola rupicola*), 232, *237*
Colobus, Zanzibar red (*Colobus kirkii*), *47*
Condor(s): Andean (*Vultur gryphus*), *242-243*;
   California (*Gymnogyps californianus*), 20, 238, *246*
Congo. *See* Zaïre
Conure, golden (*Aratinga guarouba*), *224*
Conway, William G., 18
Cormorant(s), 18, 189; Galápagos flightless
   (*Nannopterum harrisi*), *200*
Cornell University, 238
Costa Rica, 230
Coto Doñana Reserve (Spain), 241
Cougar, Florida (*Felis concolor coryi*), *85*
Cousteau, Jacques, 17
Crane(s), 212-213, *214-215*, 217; Japanese (*Grus
   japonensis*), *214-215*; Mississippi sandhill (*Grus
   canadensis pulla*), 212, 217; whooping (*Grus
   americana*), 212, *213*
Crocodile(s), 162-165; estuarine (*Crocodylus porosus*),
   162, *165*; Johnston's (*Crocodylus johnsoni*), 162, *163*;
   Nile (*Crocodylus niloticus*), 162, *164*
Crocodilians. *See* Alligator(s); Caiman(s);
   Crocodile(s); Gavial

D

Darwin, Charles, 178
Death Valley (California), 152
Deer: Key (*Odocoileus virginianus clavium*), *139*;
   swamp (*Cervus duvauceli*), 15, *127*
Dinosaurs, 26, 162, 170, 172
Dominican Republic, 36, 180
Dove, Seychelles turtle (*Streptopelia picturata
   rostrata*), 220, *226*
Duck, Laysan (*Anas laysanensis*), 190, *193*
Duiker, Jentink's (*Cephalophus jentinki*), *126*

E

Eagle(s): monkey-eating (*Pithecophaga jefferyi*), 238,
   247; southern bald (*Haliaeetus leucocephalus
   leucocephalus*), 9, 238, *245*; Spanish imperial (*Aquila
   heliaca adalberti*), *241*
East Africa, 11, 90
Ecuador, 98, 115, 160, 172
El Valle de Antón (Panama), 144

Printed in U.S.A.